History Echoes Bitcoin

Tim Niemeyer

History Echoes Bitcoin

Copyright © 2023 by Zoom Out

ISBN 979-8-9884939-0-7 (paperback)
ISBN 979-8-9884939-1-4 (ebook)

All illustrations created by DALL-E

Table of Contents

Praise for History Echoes Bitcoin

"LOVE the way the historical context is woven into each section of the book. The writing style is very approachable."
~ Blue Collar Bitcoin Podcast

"Tim is a treasured voice within the Bitcoin education movement. By telling history's hidden stories, Tim simplifies why Bitcoin matters. The future of money is buried within this unconventional history book. Start digging!"
~ Daniel Hershberger, Bitcoin Is Better

"There will be many examples to use as teaching tools to explain bitcoin to people. Nicely done and a unique angle that has not been covered."
~ Elizabeth Elaine, Bitcoin in the Lou

"Brief, powerful, really meta-level serious."
~ Anonymous

"The relevant and accessible examples make Tim's book a great way to learn about Bitcoin... and history."
~ Hector Alvero, Rhino Bitcoin

"I didn't know anything about Bitcoin, but I still liked the book!"
~ Kathy Sperry, mother of the author

Acknowledgments

As with life, few goals are accomplished by individuals unconnected from the resources and support provided by family and friends. I am no different. The following people have been critical in helping me achieve goals personally and professionally. To the love of my life, Cara, for her continued connection, attention, and affection. My children, Wes and Eleanor, for their unconditional love and giving me the motivation to be the best version of myself. To my mother and father for receiving their combined gifts and guidance along the way. To my not too shabby friend, Dave, for allowing me to explain how he can pay for diapers with bitcoin. To Danni for sharing her limitless talents. To Dan and my friends at Lincolnland Bitcoin for being part of my rabbit hole journey. To Reid, Rachel, and Tommy for their input along the way.

To Mark Maraia for mentoring me through the publishing process. There are few people I know that are equally knowledgeable over a wide range of disciplines as well as generous with their time. To Joakim Book for his attention to detail, professionalism, and insights. He made the editing process fun and mentally stimulating. To the team at Bitcoin Magazine for helping me find my voice. To the following fellow plebs for providing keen insights early in the process — Hector Alvero, Steven Sperry, Rob O'Keefe, Captain Sidd, Elizabeth Elaine, Leon Wankum, Tim Ruyle, and General Kenobi. To Peter St Onge and Conor Chepenik for allowing me to slide into their DMs for a quote.

There are so many people that I've learned from along the way. Too many to name all. Here are a few Bitcoiners particularly influential in helping shape my understanding: Andreas Antonopoulos, Jeff Booth, Saifedean Ammous, Gigi, Robert Breedlove, Knut Svanholm, Guy Swann, Vijay Boyapati, Preston Pysh, Peter McCormack, Natalie Brunell, Stephan Livera, Michael Saylor, Alex Gladstein, Parker Lewis, Tomer Strolight, Lyn Alden, Jack Mallers, Greg Foss, Anil Patel, TIP_NZ, and, of course Satoshi and Hal.

Introduction

Since you have taken the time to start reading this book, at one point or another you have probably wondered what bitcoin actually is. Is it simply a volatile asset? Is it a wasteful way to store wealth? Is it even backed by anything? All these questions and more are necessary first steps to understanding. Unfortunately, because it is a paradigm shift in how we think about how we own and transfer value, Bitcoin cannot succinctly be placed into a simple soundbite suitable for complete comprehension. This is because it connects so many aspects of life: cryptography, computer science, distributed systems, open source software, network effects, game theory, economics, monetary theory, energy production, geopolitics, governance, history, human rights, philosophy, human psychology, and personal responsibility, just to name a few.

Asking a bunch of people to describe Bitcoin is like asking them to describe an elephant while standing in front of its various body parts. One might describe the tusk where others might focus on the trunk and yet others would describe the tail, and so on. Similarly, some might see Bitcoin as a way to promote freedom in authoritarian countries where another sees it as a green way to balance electrical grids and bootstrap renewable resources. Others think of it as financial freedom, a way to opt out of the maddening debasement of a country's currency where others see it as the ultimate tool to secure property rights in the digital age. Many living without stable financial services see it as a cheaper, easier, and safer way to conduct remittances. None of these are wrong;

---

[1] David Hume, *An Enquiry Into Human Understanding*, 90.

they're all accurate, and each can coexist inside the protocol of Bitcoin. To clarify, Bitcoin with a capital "B" refers the protocol, but bitcoin with a lowercase "b" refers to the asset.

Unfortunately, Bitcoin is still seen by many as something untested and/or unnecessary. Some even consider it dangerous. In 2017, the World Economic Foundation predicted, "In 2020 Bitcoin will consume more power than the world does today."[2] A quick fact-checking note... they were off by a skosh: as of 2023, Bitcoin's global share of electricity/energy consumption is less than a fraction of one percent.[3] Another amusing example was when a communist Chinese economist surmised in 2021 that, if bitcoin is widely adopted, "We're all going to die...."[4] One might wonder if there was fire and brimstone present during that declaration.

Those who feed the FUD (fear, uncertainty, and doubt) may have deep and nuanced understanding of various fields of thought, but they lack the crucial mental proof of work required to comprehend the true nature of Bitcoin. While these people may have authority in their specific areas of study, that does not give them the necessary information to comprehend a completely new paradigm, an invention in the way humans transact not only digital value but also how we conduct ourselves fairly and ethically on a global scale. Blindly following these people have led much of society to mischaracterize, misunderstand, and/or underappreciate Bitcoin's immense potential as an upgrade over the current system.

Furthermore, many of Bitcoin's naysayers are incentivized to see its demise. It's similar to Kodak's resistance to the development of digital photography. The music industry's use of lawsuits attempted to thwart the rise of online music sharing services such as Napster. The taxi industry attempted to regulate away the development of ride

---

[2] Adam Jezard, "Bitcoin Will Consume."
[3] Cambridge Centre for Alternative Finance, "Bitcoin Network Power Demand."
[4] Kevin Helms "Chinese Economist."

sharing services like Uber and Lyft. Interestingly, one of Bitcoin's biggest detractors, economist Paul Krugman stated in 1998, "By 2005 or so, it will become clear that the Internet's impact on the economy has been no greater than the fax machine's."[5] It is true that many industries will be upended by Bitcoin's disruptive technology. It's important to remember that it's natural and even healthy during evolution for older, now useless systems to fall by the wayside. Not to disparage the once-proud occupation, but do we still need elevator operators?

It is my contention in this book that this short-sighted thinking by self-imposed, potentially at-risk experts obfuscates the virtuous properties that constitute Bitcoin. Independently, these properties have been helping humanity develop for centuries. Throughout the following chapters, it would be beneficial for the reader to set aside any preconceptions about what they think Bitcoin actually is. Also, there is no need to get a computer science degree or try to understand the implications of cryptography applied to geopolitics. Rather, just realize how the properties presented are ethically and morally superior on their individual merits.

After you've pondered each property in isolation, only then can you start to fully visualize a world in which Bitcoin is a step-change improvement on the current, broken system. A quote, often attributed to American architect, systems theorist, writer, designer, inventor, philosopher, and futurist, Buckminster Fuller goes, "You never change things by fighting the existing reality. To change something, build a new model that makes the existing model obsolete."[6] It is my belief that the existing monetary fiat standard is broken, which makes it easier for people in positions of power to manipulate the system to their benefit. As you will hopefully realize, our current monetary system is the antithesis of the properties discussed in this book. It is therefore necessary for us to understand the virtues Bitcoin provides so we can embrace and promote the already widespread adoption underway.

---

[5] Paul Krugman, "Most Economists' Predictions."
[6] Elke Hackle, "You Never Change Things."

Before we get too far ahead of ourselves, let's take a moment to realize the technology that constitutes Bitcoin is not *new* per se. While the protocol has only been operational since 2009, decades of research, development, and iterations have gone into forming much of Bitcoin's inner workings. As with many inventions, they are forged by the fire of countless previous attempts. Cypherpunks are the modern day metalworkers striving to mold an imperishable digital system of value transfer. Only after many failed attempts have we finally arrived at a viable and stable solution.

Bitcoin's Prehistory

With the advent of TCP/IP in 1974, cryptography had discovered a brand new method of metallurgy. Soon followed Merkle Trees in 1980, which is used to verify stored data between shared computers. In the early 1980s, David Chaum created "Untraceable Electronic Mail, Return Addresses, and Digital Pseudonyms"[7] as well as "Blind Signature for Untraceable Payments."[8] Sandwiched in time between them were the creation of elliptical curve technology that makes it extremely difficult to obtain private keys when given a public key. In 1989, David Chaum founded the short-lived Digicash, an early form of electronic payment.[9]

The 1990s brought further improvements such as PGP (Pretty Good Privacy), digital time-stamps, not to mention Tim Berners-Lee's World Wide Web in 1992. With the cypherpunks movement gaining traction, further projects attempted to perfect digital value transfer in the form

---

[7] David Chaum, "Untraceable Electronic Mail."
[8] David Chaum, "Blind Signatures."
[9] Finn Brunton, *Digital Cash.*

of 1996's e-Gold. Wei Dai's b-money, and Nick Szabo's Bit Gold in 1998.[10]

The 2000s brought us lookup retrieval services in the form of distributed hash tables, peer-to-peer file sharing such as BitTorrent, and the legendary Hal Finney's Reusable Proof-of-Work in 2004, which has found its rightful home as Bitcoin's consensus algorithm.[11] By the time 2008 came around, much of the technology found in pseudonymous creator, Satoshi Nakamoto's, Bitcoin was already well established. While Satoshi added two very crucial new developments, solving the Byzantine Generals Problem and creating the difficulty adjustment, their greatest accomplishment was incorporating all the previous developments into one simple but beautiful digital monetary protocol.[12] Satoshi perfectly channeled Isaac Newton's famous saying, "If I have seen further it is by standing on the shoulders of giants."[13]

If none of that made sense, it's okay. What percent of the population can explain the intricacies of how satellite communication works? Still, we all use smartphones. To appreciate Bitcoin, you don't need to know how all the aforementioned technological advancements work independently or collectively. The point is — Bitcoin is not some new-fangled get-rich-quick pyramid scheme like many ignorant pundits would have you to believe. It is the brainchild of decades of research and development. It's similar to the need for humans to discover fire and create the wheel before we could invent internal combustion engines. Okay, enough techy-nerd stuff...

---

[10] Brunton, *Digital Cash*; Aaron van Wirdum, "The Genesis Files: How David Chaim's eCash spawned a cypherpunk dream," *Bitcoin Magazine*.

[11] Hal Finney, "RPOW - Reusable Proofs of Work." Sjors Provoost, *Bitcoin: A Work in Progress: Technical Innovations from the Trenches*.

[12] Jeff Booth, "Finding Signal in a Noisy World," *Bitcoin Magazine*.

[13] Robert Merton, *On the Shoulders of Giants: A Shandean Postscript*.

The Properties

Let us now take a trip through history while we focus on the properties that are represented in Bitcoin. Of those are permissionlessness, gaining consensus, decentralization, trust minimization, censorship resistance, open source collaboration, immutability, and scarcity. Each one has shown throughout history to be beneficial to mankind. Each one has moved humanity forward in one way or another. Every historical example or non-example provided in this book serves as a lesson for us to either choose to learn from or ignore. This book aims to show how the properties that give Bitcoin its value are each individually beneficial and have helped shape positive aspects of society.

Permissionlessness

"Sign, sign, everywhere a sign.
Blockin' out the scenery, breakin' my mind.
Do this, don't do that, can't you read the sign?"
~ Five Man Electrical Band

One definition of permission is "authorization granted to do something; formal consent."[14] Consent is when approval is given to another party. Therefore, consent and permission are intrinsically linked. Throughout history, there have been countless instances where voluntary exchange, the granting of access or respect of refusal, is not honored. Unfortunately, many instances have gone so far past the point of permission and consent that they ignore the natural right of autonomy (ex - people have free will and the deprivation of this right is immoral).

As Robert Heinlein wrote in his classic 1966 science fiction novel, *The Moon Is a Harsh Mistress*, "I will accept any rules that you feel necessary to your freedom. I am free, no matter what rules surround me. If I find them tolerable, I tolerate them; if I find them too obnoxious, I break them. I am free because I know that I alone am morally responsible for everything I do."[15] In that spirit, we must strive for a higher level of autonomy, provided we maintain the mindset of the Golden Rule, "Do unto others as you would like them to do to you."

While everyone has a preference for how much or how little they believe permission should be woven into our societal fabric, the fact remains that human nature tends to gravitate towards power and control when opportunities arise. The following episodes in history illuminate what is possible when one group or class of people assert unchecked authority over another, regardless of perceived ethics or morality. It is

---

[14] Dictionary.com "Permission."
[15] Robert Heinlein, *The Moon is a Harsh Mistress*, 65.

necessary for us to meditate on these in order to see the positives that permissionless protocols provide.

The Protestant Reformation

Back in the 1600s, many Christians were fed up with the perceived authority the Catholic Church held over its constituents. For example, Martin Luther challenged the Church's doctrine that the Pope, not the Bible, was the ultimate spiritual authority. This is in addition to the church's practice of selling indulgences, where one could pay the church to forgive their sins. Nice little racket they had going, eh? On October 31, 1517, Luther historically flexed his permissionlessness nature by setting off what is now known as the Protestant Reformation. In a bold act, Luther nailed his 95 theses to Castle Church in Wittenberg, Germany. These were arguments that the Bible owned religious authority, as opposed to the clergy, and that humans may reach salvation through faith in God as opposed to the act of good deeds.

In proper authoritarian form, the Church's response was to declare Luther a heretic, someone who does not conform to generally accepted beliefs or practices. Thus he was promptly excommunicated; basically he was kicked out of the Church. The good news for Luther is that he had already realized he did not need the permission of men in fancy hats to worship his God. This led to the split of Christianity into Catholics and Protestants (originating from the word *protest*). Imagine that: a group of people are forced through the absence of consent to follow an arbitrary set of rules, and they stand up for themselves and exert their natural autonomy.[16]

One of the greatest benefits resulting from the Reformation was the feeling of empowerment the common man received. Prior to the Reformation, many Europeans were dependent upon the educated and entitled class to provide them with answers and guidance for religious questions and other aspects of life.[17] It's not just a coincidence that once the concept of autonomy was introduced to the equation and the ill-perceived veil of permission was lifted, human flourishing was able to spread.

Christ's sinlessness was his proof of work, allowing fallible humans to free themselves from the shackles of authority via a virtuous blueprint. Placing the good word above the word of man allowed everyone the self-permission to more intimately walk with God. The slave no longer needed the slave owner's permission to be free of thought, because they now had a higher order of ideals to follow. This is similar to how Bitcoin's pristine ledger provides freedom for individuals to determine value without needing to ask for access to the current authority's permissioned ledger or their viewpoint on what is valuable.

---

[16] William Bernstein, *The Delusions of Crowds*.
[17] Sasha Becker, Steven Praff, and Jared Rubin, "Causes and Consequences of the Protestant Reformation."

Jim Crow Laws

Let's now take a stroll down legal-doesn't-mean-moral boulevard…. Beginning in the late 1800s, southern states in the US began legally enforcing racial segregation. This was in reaction to the post-Civil War reconstruction resulting from the Emancipation Proclamation of 1863. Like a bully who got bullied, Southern states didn't appreciate the authority the federal government was imposing, so they imposed their own perceived authority over the African Americans living inside their borders. Although former slaves were given certain permissions thanks to the Emancipation Proclamation (abolition of slavery, citizenship, and the right to vote), the US Supreme Court legitimized this segregation under the "separate but equal" clause as a result of 1896's Plessy v. Ferguson.[18]

Thus the era of Jim Crow laws began, where states and local authorities introduced in the southern United States that effectively shoved African Americans squarely back to second-class citizen status. "Jim Crow" was a pejorative term based on a stock character done in blackface in minstrel shows throughout the United States, which reinforced racial prejudice. Despite the glaring issue of these

---

[18] History.com, "Plessy v. Ferguson."

permissions not being moral in the first place, Jim Crow laws basically erased any political progress through the revocation of legal permissions that African Americans had gained during the Reconstruction.

Although the Thirteenth Amendment of 1865 legally abolished slavery, the disenfranchisement occurring from Jim Crow laws reverberated throughout the African American community. White lawmakers, attempting to codify permissions in a post-slavery South, began writing what was known as the Black Codes, which included the right to marry and the right to own property. These permissions were countered with the inability to own firearms, forced labor contracts for extremely little wages, and withdrawing their constitutional right to vote. Black Codes were basically slavery disguised as legal permissions.[19]

The Fourteenth Amendment of 1868 granted full citizenship to anyone born in the United States regardless of slavery. The Fifteenth Amendment of 1870 stated that US citizens shall not be denied the right to vote based on race, color, or previous state of slavery. Interesting sidenote, this permission was only provided to men; women didn't receive the right to vote until the Nineteenth Amendment in 1919 and 1920.

Many more decades passed until society was able to shift the entrenched Overton window during the time of Jim Crow. The Civil Rights movement of the 1960s illuminated the hypocrisies permeating our culture. Despite all the gains since, African Americans still face numerous structural challenges created throughout previous generations with regards to legal permissions. Please note that I am by no means minimizing the overwhelming atrocities African Americans faced during the times of Jim Crow, not to mention throughout the era of slavery. I believe all we can do is learn the lessons from the past and try to create a fair and compassionate society moving forward by creating permissionless social systems.

---

[19] Vanessa Holloway, *Black Rights in the Reconstruction Era*.

Executive Order 6102

Executive Order 6102 was a presidential order issued by Franklin D. Roosevelt in 1933 that demanded Americans surrender their personal holdings of gold. This confiscation by the government was in response to the stock market crash of the late 1920s and the Great Depression in the 1930s. Years of economic contraction crippled the average American's financial situation. The US government felt compelled to intervene in the form of revoking the perceived permission of their population to hold their store of value in the form of gold. This allowed the rule-makers to create a buttload of money in order to alleviate the constraints on the Federal Reserve through price inflation and increase the velocity of money in the economy.[20]

While the benevolent FDR generously allowed each citizen to save a few troy ounces (unit of measure used for weighing precious metals) of gold bullion as well as receive $20.67 per ounce exchanged, once the Gold Reserve Act of 1934 was signed, the exchange rate ballooned to $35 per ounce. So the government handcuffed the population's

---

[20] Barry Eichengreen, *Golden Fetters*.

ability to save, stole from its constituents, then profited from the ordeal. Oh, and if any citizen didn't comply with their demands, they'd be fined $10,000 and face up to 10 years in prison.[21] That's a fine how-do-you-do. So in one fell swoop, citizens' ability to save was demolished.

This move wasn't unprecedented, though. In the fourth century, Ancient Romans made it illegal to trade gold at anything other than the emperor's fixed rate. The eighteenth-century Brits suspended the convertibility of banknotes into gold to prevent a bank run during the Napoleonic Wars. Just a few decades prior to Executive Order 6102, then President Woodrow Wilson made it illegal to hoard gold during World War I.[22] Around that same time, the Soviets banned private gold ownership in order to nationalize it.

The desire by the few to manipulate the many into actions that benefit the few is a story as old as time. This specific overreach of rich men in suits restricting working-class folks' ability to store wealth was just another lesson from history that well-connected people will use any emergency to usurp more control over those on the lower rungs of society. It's just easier for them to revoke permissions during times of turmoil. Like the quote attributed to Winston Churchill goes, "Never let a good crisis go to waste."[23]

---

[21] Henry Mark Holzer, "How Americans Lost Their Right to Own Gold."

[22] Leland Crabbe, "The International Gold Standard."

[23] Melissa Aronczyk, "Brands and the Pandemic."

The Berlin Wall

Want to visit your family? Too bad... if you were a German in the mid-1900s. From the early 1960s, a barrier, a physical manifestation of the refusal of permission, was created between East and West Germany. Lingering tensions from World War II led the Allied powers to split control of Germany between the democratic West and the communist East. This led to the physical restriction of movement and trade in the form of what was known as the "Iron Curtain."

Rather quickly, East Germans began to leave for less oppressive locations, and the authoritarian regime reacted by officially closing the border. A fence with barbed wire was constructed. That didn't stop the exodus as people jumped over the fence or traveled around it. To stop the outward flow of the government's property... er... human beings, a blockade spanning the entire country was built. Along the border between East and West Berlin, the blockade was topped by an unclimbable smooth pipe, covered in barbed fencing, surrounded by spike strips, guard dogs, landmines, and watchtowers; the powers that be made it nearly impossible for their workforce to leave.

If that wasn't enough, one hundred meters of land was stripped, and a fence with barbed wire was placed at the other end. This was affectionately known as the "Death Strip" where guards were given... permission... to shoot anyone who crossed. While some still were able to defect, countless numbers of families were separated, and many relationships sadly and abruptly ended.[24]

Did that stop the people who exercised their free will? Heck no. Nearly five thousand East Germans fled across the Berlin Wall; millions more escaped East Germany during Communist reign from 1949 to 1990. Some defected while traveling abroad. Others swam across canals. Some flew in hot air balloons to escape.[25] Others dug escape tunnels before *The Shawshank Redemption* made it cool. There was even a report of a brave soul crashing a stolen tank through the wall to escape. While many lost their lives in their attempt to live freely, all who attempted displayed the positive attribute of free will in the face of tyranny. Permission be damned, especially when the governing body didn't have the moral right to impose it in the first place.

As time went on, families were allowed to cross the arbitrary dividing line and gather. The Basic Treaty of 1972 made that possible, but it was far from permissionless. As authoritarian governments do to maintain control while discouraging progress, the Communist regime created an onerous system of paperwork and documentation for families to meet, not to mention even being charged a fee in the process. That's right; you had to pay to receive permission to see a loved one.

Thankfully, by the 1980s democracy in formerly Communist European countries began gaining popularity. In 1987, then US President Ronald Regan famously demanded, "Mr. Gorbachev, tear down this wall!" The East German authorities attempted to lighten the restrictions for permission, but that fueled the fire of free-flowing humanity. By 1989, free people were fed up and started gathering at the

---

[24] Patrick Major, *Behind the Berlin Wall*.
[25] Leslie Colitt, "Escape from East Berlin."

wall in protest.[26] Overwhelmed guards eventually opened the gates while citizens began destroying the wall with whatever tools they could find. In the end, East and West Germany were reunited. Parts of the wall still stand. We can use this as a lesson that while many will try to impose a sense of authority over us, but as long as we are not aggressing on the rights of others, it is our moral right to move freely without the permission of others.

A Tale of Two Koreas

After centuries of warring factions attempting to garner control over the Korean peninsula, a solution presented itself in 1945. At the end of World War II, Korea officially split along the 38th parallel to create North Korea, occupied by the communist Soviets, and South Korea, which was occupied by the democratic United States. By 1948, the Democratic People's Republic of North Korea was established as was South Korea, also known as the Republic of Korea. This agreement didn't last long. By 1950, Soviet-backed North Koreans invaded South Korea in what is now known as the Korean War. This war lasted until

---

[26] Hope Harrison, "Five Myths About the Berlin Wall."

1953 when the demilitarized zone (DMZ) was established demarcating a clear dividing line between the two countries. From there, both Koreas took their own path in regards to permission. North Koreans chose the authoritarian and communist path while South Korea took the path of democracy and freedom. The differences in cultures since this split are illuminating and send a clear message as to how we all should think globally and act locally.[27]

Want to travel? If you're North Korean, you can fly out of their one and only international airport. This one-terminal airport allows access to only two airlines — Air China and North Korea's own Air Koryo, which is the only one-star rated airline in the world, receiving close to six thousand international passengers a year. In contrast, Seoul, South Korea hosts one of the biggest, busiest, and cleanest airports in the world with an estimated fifty million yearly international travelers flying on sixty different airlines.

None of that matters though because, if you were North Korean, your chances of receiving a passport is slim to none. Only the most well-connected in their communist society get permission to obtain this rarity. Even worse, most North Koreans need permission to leave their own town, let alone travel outside their country's border. South Koreans, on the other hand, have one of the most powerful passports in the world allowing travel to nearly everywhere in the world.[28]

Do you love the nightlife? You got to boogie? You can actually go to a karaoke bar or two in North Korea… provided you're part of the privileged class. The best the peasants can muster are speakeasy-type house parties in their rural shanties where they listen to South Korean K-Pop music under the shadow of potential punishment. South Korea offers a stark contrast rivaling that of large downtown nightlife found in the United States.

Wanna make your house a home? Too bad. Because North Korea owns all the land, its citizens are assigned housing by the government.

---

[27] William Stueck, "The Korean War."
[28] Michael Seth, *A History of Korea.*

Most of the countryside is without heat or proper plumbing. Conversely, South Koreans are free to choose where they live with affordable prices compared to other countries in southeast Asia.

If you're an aspiring journalist, you may want to steer clear of North Korea unless you enjoy regurgitating communist propaganda and only speaking positively about elected leaders. If you stray from the script, you might receive prison time or be sentenced to hard labor. All South Koreans on the other hand have the benefit of exercising their wacky rights of freedom of speech and freedom of the press. Suck on that, Kim Jong Un.

While both Koreas claim free healthcare, the differences couldn't be more stark. Firstly, North Korean healthcare is not easily accessible to those serfs on the lower rungs of society. Even the wealthy and connected class receive poor-quality care with many hospitals operating without heat or electricity. The biggest difference in healthcare is that all South Koreans, regardless of wealth or clout, have access to their healthcare system, which is light-years ahead of its neighbor to the north.

Hey, peasant, want to travel to shop in a North Korean supermarket? Tough shit. You at least have permission to grow your own food, which is gradually becoming a thing of the past in many developed, authoritarian-ish countries. Despite that, the *Wall Street Journal* reported that 41% of the North Korean population is undernourished. One shocking point is that meat is hard to come by in North Korea while it is abundant to the south of their border. In addition, South Korean cuisine is well-known throughout the world and access to affordable international ingredients is common.

North Korean education is mandatory and rife with propaganda. Every classroom must display portraits of the dear leaders on their walls, literally worshiping them as gods. While they do have universities, you guessed it, only the rich kids get to go. But that's okay because every man in North Korea has to serve a mandatory ten-year tour in the military. That number is seven years for women. To no surprise, South Korea boasts being one of the most educated countries in the world. Everyone is granted permission to attend, and the majority go on to higher levels of education.

Permissionlessness

*"I sought the advice and cooperation from all those around me,
but not permission."*
~ Muhammad Ali

All of these episodes in history stem from the lack of consent. One could argue that the absence of obtaining permission is still a concern in modern society. Many people in power use justifications for their overreach while ignoring basic human decency. Some might suggest these overreaches are still prevalent, maybe even increasing. It led Ayn Rand in 1964 to observe, "We are fast approaching the stage of the ultimate inversion: the stage where the government is free to do anything it pleases, while the citizens may act only by permission; which is the stage of the darkest periods of human history, the stage of rule by brute force."[29]

Think of permission as a spectrum. The further a culture travels to the highly permissioned side, the worse the leaders treat their constituents. Rarely does one person or a small group truly *know* what is best for everyone. Conversely, the further a culture travels to a permissionless side of the spectrum, the more free-flowing and flourishing a culture can become. Granted, this is not to promote full-out, anything-goes anarchy. Systems must have checks and balances in place in order to respect private property rights for example. This will be discussed further in future chapters.

The overarching problem with most of these examples is that the ruleset is mediated between both entities; they are each able to change the rules of engagement to benefit themselves. This inherently expresses the fallibility of our current system of interactions. This protocol ignores the natural right of opting into or out of voluntary interaction. If these episodes in history have taught us anything, it is

---

[29] Ayn Rand, "The Nature of Government."

that humanity would flourish with the advent of a permissionless protocol that mediates voluntary interaction, which is ideally abstracted away from the physical realm. Only then can we have competing systems built upon it, which would allow for voluntary choice. Said differently, the problem with communism (or socialism, or any -ism for that matter) is the lack of choice.

Ultimately, a voluntary society has yet to scale due to the lack of a global rule set that isn't inherently compulsory. The key here is that all solutions thus far have been overwhelmingly permissioned. Regardless of justifications given, those who grant or deny permission are allowed to express their morals onto others; they are just as subject to the natural pull of human incentives as anyone. If we've learned anything from these instances in history, it is that we should place a high value on protocols that are permissionless. Martin Luther King, Jr. offered the framework to achieve this goal by stating "Freedom is never voluntarily given by the oppressor; it must be demanded by the oppressed."[30]

---

[30] Martin Luther King, Jr. "Letter From Birmingham Jail, Alabama, 16 April 1963."

Gaining Consensus

"Consensus is the negation of leadership."[31]
~ Margaret Thatcher

One of the many attributes that makes the human race advanced is the ability to consider others' viewpoints and perspectives when making decisions that affect more than just oneself. This protocol of making decisions in a group setting is known as consensus. The word consensus originates from the Latin word *cōnsēnsus*, which translates to agreement, accordance, and unanimity.[32]

The difficulty with gaining consensus is that everyone rightfully has their own interests at heart. This leads to the concept of game theory, which is the study of participants' behavior in strategic situations. Game theory has multiple applications across wide-ranging fields. In addition to mathematics, game theory is used in logic, systems science, and computer science. One famous thought example in game theory is the prisoner's dilemma, where two completely rational agents must choose either to cooperate with their partner for mutual benefit or betray their partner for individual reward. When given the chance to play the game over and again, greedy strategies tend to do poorly over time while more altruistic strategies do better. This revelation suggested how decision-making behavior evolved to be more altruistic when compared to purely selfish behaviors.[33]

By analyzing the ways humanity attempted to achieve consensus, we can see more clearly the need for applying them into society. Charlie Munger once said, "show me the incentive and I'll show you

---

[31] Los Angeles Times Editors, "Margaret Thatcher: The Lady is Not Made For Ducking a Tough Question."
[32] Wiktionary, "Consensus."
[33] Robert Axelrod, *The Evolution of Cooperation.*

---

the outcome."[34] Understanding how these instances are made based on individuals and their incentives helps illuminate the issues.

---

[34] Jill Gunter, "Crypto's Bad Incentives Are Dying."

Ignaz Semmelweis

In the mid-nineteenth century, an aspiring doctor made an ominous observation. Upon securing a position at Vienna General Hospital, Ignaz Semmelweis grew troubled at the growing number of deaths occuring in one of the maternity wards he was overseeing. The ward in which established doctors oversaw many patients, the rate of childbed fever — where mothers were dying after childbirth — was a staggering sixteen percent. In the other maternity ward, the one led by midwives and students that served the underprivileged, the rate of maternal death hovered around only two percent. As a good scientist should, he began collecting data. After multiple attempts to isolate the problem, Ignaz finally found the problem.[35]

During that time in history, the majority of the medical profession believed illnesses were caused by bad air or even evil spirits. Semmleweis finally noticed the esteemed doctors, the ones in the ward with the high rate of childbed fever at the time, were leaving the morgue

---

[35] Carter and Carter, *Childbed Fever: A Scientific Biography of Ignaz Semmelweis.*

after finishing autopsies and heading straight to the maternity ward to deliver babies… without washing their hands in between. Without knowing the exact mechanism — germ theory was yet to be invented — Ignaz Semmleweis had a clue as to why countless women were unnecessarily dying after childbirth.

Thrilled by this discovery, Semmelweis promptly shared his findings with his peers. One would think this is the end of a happy story. Unfortunately, the medical fraternity rejected his thesis. After receiving ridicule, the outraged Ignaz wrote to medical journals basically calling the medical establishment murderers for their negligence. Despite his swift fall to pariah status, Semmelweis continued doing what he believed was right.

It wasn't until a colleague of his died from an open puncture wound received while conducting an autopsy that Ignaz finally had a connection. This offered proof of physically transmitting what we now know as germs. He immediately developed a hand-washing protocol using chlorinated lime and ordered all personnel wash their hands before female examination. In addition, he recommended all hospital instruments be cleaned in the same solution. In one year, the maternal mortality rate plummeted down to below two percent.

Despite the overwhelming results, Semmelweis was considered an extremist and an outcast simply because he did not have an acceptable scientific explanation. Desperate to save lives (and possibly his social standing in the medical community), Semmelweis began handing out pamphlets in the streets to women urging them to request doctors wash their hands. Little helped move the social consensus, which was controlled by the scientific establishment. Many doctors were offended that they should be considered the ones who should be held responsible. The consensus of Vienna General Hospital's medical professionals effectively ostracized Ignaz.

Semmelweis dejectedly returned to his childhood home of Budapest to revive his medical career. Although he couldn't find a similar job, he took a volunteer physician position and swiftly eradicated much of the disease present with his radical hand-washing idea. Still, his ideas weren't respected. He was even accused of being mentally unstable. The stonewalling by the established science community sent Semmelweis into a deep depression. Twenty years after his discovery, Ignaz was committed to an insane asylum. He died two weeks later... from an infection of a wound received after a struggle with the guards.[36]

Despite an organization's credentials and experience, it still has blind spots for good ideas. Either a concept is seemingly too ahead of its time, it just contains too much of a paradigm shift for a specific group to comprehend, or the group would look downright silly (not to mention possibly liable) if the outsider opinion was allowed room to flourish. To that last point, there's something that needs to be said about a group's decision to a situation carrying a portion of the group's DNA. As was stated in this chapter's introduction, all groups are made up of individuals with their own incentives as well as biases. Regardless of how solid a group's ability to come to consensus is, there will always be human fallibility baked into each decision.

[36] John Galbraith Simmons, *Doctors and Discoveries*; Nicholas Kadar, "Rediscovering Ignaz Philipp Semmelweis (1818–1865)," 35.

Grand Council of the Six Nations

One of the oldest participatory democracies in history was the Haudenosaunee, translated to People of the Longhouse. It was formed sometime between the twelfth and fifteenth century based on oral accounts. The French called them the Iroquois Confederacy. Also known as the people of the Six Nations, these tribes lived in what is now New York and the adjacent, southeastern part of Canada. The tribes were (geographically from west to east) Seneca, Cayuga, Onondaga, Oneida, and the Mohawk. The sixth nation known as the Tuscarora later joined them in the early eighteenth century.

Up until their alliance was formed, many wars were fought over territory and resources. What was obviously missing was a system in place where each nation could live in harmony. One of the early founders of the Iroquois Confederacy, Hiawatha, met a native indian prophet known as The Peacemaker. While no one knew his true identity, The Peacemaker offered guidance and a system to peacefully gain consensus. This consensus mechanism was dubbed "The Great

Plan of Peace."[37] Has a nice ring to it, huh? Over time, alliances were formed where each tribe would remain autonomous in regards to their own affairs while also helping defend each other from outside attackers. Imagine that... let everyone live their own lives while also defending each others' property rights. Seems legit.

The steps required to gain consensus were not easily obtained. No "executive orders," lol. First, while sitting around the council fire, elder brothers from the Mohawk and Seneca tribes would need to gain consensus. Then, those ideas would be passed to the younger brothers of the Cayuga and Oneida tribes while the elder brothers listened. When both elder and younger brothers agreed, the Onondaga tribe, which were keepers of the council fire, would give their judgment. All council decisions needed to be unanimous, thus always working toward consensus. If consensus was not unanimous at any point in the process, the council had to be restarted. Finally, once all tribes agreed, consensus was obtained. An interesting aspect of their consensus rule set was that the women were the ones to elect the men into council leadership roles. If the men did not do their job well enough, the women would vote them out.[38]

In the mid eighteenth century, English colonies on the east coast began attempting to develop their own system of governance apart from British rule. Their problem was similar in that each colony wanted control over making the rules, but they all wanted protection from British authoritarianism. Having heard of the Iroquois League's peaceful consensus, Benjamin Franklin invited the council in 1765 at the New Albany Convention to describe their peaceful system of governance to the soon-to-be developing American government. That's right... As stated in the Congressional Record in 1987, The Great Plan of Peace developed by the Haudenosaunee directly affected the formation of what is now the Constitution of the United States of

---

[37] Tony Tekaroniake Evans, "How the Iroquois Confederacy Was Formed."
[38] Nancy Shoemaker, "The Rise or Fall of Iroquois Women," 40.

America.[39] The overarching lesson learned from this episode in history is that true ethical and moral governance is obtained when local autonomy, property rights, and the consent of the governed are respected.

---

[39] Mike Lee, *Written Out of History*; Bruce Johansen, *Forgotten Founders*.

Munich Agreement

Let's face it. Sometimes we're not the biggest dog in the fight. As Kenny Rogers said, "You gotta know when to hold 'em, know when to fold 'em, know when to talk away, and know when to run." When a decision needs to be made in those situations, sometimes you stand up for yourself, sometimes you talk it out, sometimes you might turn the other cheek, and sometimes you need to turn around and walk away. None of these possible solutions are always the right answer; every situation offers different challenges. Unfortunately, history didn't benefit when Neville Chamberlain chose to appease the bully on the block by signing the Munich Agreement of 1938 with Adolph Hitler.[40]

As Hitler was gaining political and military power in the early 1930s, most European leaders increasingly turned a blind eye. By disregarding much of the Treaty of Versailles, Hitler was able to gain top dog status in Europe; Germany was now the overwhelming power. One of Hitler's main policy goals at that time was Lebensraum, to gain greater living space for Germans. The Anschluss of 1938 seized control

---

[40] Frank Donough, *Neville Chamberlain, Appeasement, and the British Road to War,* ch. 5.

of Austria. Hitler then turned his focus to the heavily German-populated part of Czechoslovakia known as Sudetenland.

In stepped Neville Chamberlain, then Prime Minister of Great Britain. Without even considering finding consensus first with the Czechoslovakian people, Chamberlain appeased Hitler by allowing Sudetenland to be annexed by Germany. After the fact, Chamberlain returned to persuade the French and Czechoslovakian governments to accept his concession. Immediately after this consensus was formalized, now known as the Munich Agreement, Chamberlain returned home to brag in one of the most insert-foot-in-mouth moments in history by uttering that he had brought "peace for our time." Within a year, Germany invaded Poland, which marked the beginning of World War II.

Had Chamberlain listened to his critics, like Winston Churchill, he may have had a more well-rounded, thought-out strategy to employ. Churchill's famous reply to Chamberlain's chickenshit move was to not-so-clairvoyantly declare "You were given the choice between war and dishonour. You choose dishonour and you will have war."[41] It's not like Churchill was playing the optics game; he had been a vocal critic of the increasing Nazi power grab. He banged the table for faster rearmament and for Britain and other nations to stand their ground against Hitler. Churchill clearly perceived the fault in Chamberlain's consensus-seeking strategy by stating, "There never can be any absolute certainty that there will be a fight if one side is determined that it will give way completely."[42]

What can we glean from this? Was WWII all Neville Chamberlain's fault? Absolutely not. Hitler and his Nazis were the horrible people that were responsible for the atrocities. One takeaway, though, could be that decisions are best made when the most voices possible are present at the table. Granted, too many chefs and not enough cooks leads to a lackluster meal. But if one human brain can

---

[41] Telford Taylor, *Munich: The Price of Peace*, 978.
[42] Winston Churchill, "The Munich Agreement."

process roughly one hundred and twenty bits a second, imagine the potential computing power of an entire population. Try to visualize the outcome of gaining consensus in potential wartime when every human in society has an actual vote. When we let a small number of people make choices, especially spineless ones, the results could literally affect the rest of the world. Simply put, consensus reached by a few is not the consensus of the many. The more we can process the preferences and perspectives of all parties present, the more we can come to clear consensus.

Good Friday Agreement

The early twentieth century was contentious for many countries in and around the United Kingdom. Even though the Irish Free State was established in 1922, many tensions remained between the British-supporting unionists and Irish-supporting nationalists. Many unionists believed the nationalists of Northern Ireland were disloyal and were trying to force the rest of Ireland into their view of a united Ireland.

Conversely, Northern Ireland nationalists denounced the Irish unionists' desire to form a union with Great Britain.

As the decades progressed, violence between the two sides grew more and more intense, especially in Northern Ireland. Thousands of deaths, over half of which were civilians, crescendoed into what became affectionately known as "The Troubles," starting in the 1960s. Guerilla warfare tactics spread throughout the land. Numerous bombing, even in shopping centers, were carried out by the Irish Republican Army (IRA). Public shootings were common for both sides with the "Bloody Sunday" massacre of 1972 being the most notable. This is when thirteen unarmed civil rights protesters were shot by British soldiers. Assassinations of royal family members were commonplace. Both sides carried out punishment attacks where they would either beat or shoot their own community members under the suspicion of being crossed. Property damage was widespread, especially during riots of parades and marches.[43]

By the 1980s, many ceasefires, proposals, and compromises were declared but were rarely successful; the words and actions of current government officials were useless. Even the United States attempted to mediate by sitting in on the talks. Finally, in 1998 an agreement was made. The multiparty agreement involved most of Northern Ireland's political parties as well as the British and Irish governments. This agreement allowed Northern Ireland to self-govern in addition to a "power-sharing" component for each party. One main aspect included in the agreement was the concept of governmental consent; one country could not arbitrarily pass laws without the consent of the others. Sovereignty and governance were respected.

In regards to gaining consensus, one of the most important aspects of this agreement was that voters' opinions were valued. Multiple referendums were held. The Northern Ireland citizens were asked if they supported the multiparty agreement. The Irish citizens were asked if they consented to changes to their constitution in order to seal the deal. If either set of constituents declined, the agreement would not go into effect. By respecting each group's perspectives and desires, consensus was gained with the 1998 Good Friday Agreement.

---

[43] Graham Dawson et al., *The Northern Ireland Troubles in Britain.*

Byzantine Generals Problem

Originally conceived by computer scientist Robert Shostak in 1978, the Byzantine Generals Problem, originally called "interactive consistency problem,"[44] attempted to reach consensus between multiple connected computers. The thought experiment asked the question: How can one make sure that multiple entities separated by distance are in absolute full agreement before taking an action? Basically, how does one guarantee consensus? This problem has plagued theorists for decades.

In terms of the historical representation of this thought experiment, imagine you are one of four Byzantine generals having the enemy surrounded in a forthcoming battle. If all of the generals' armies attack at the same time, they surely will overpower their opponent. If they attack at different times, their success would not be as certain. Mind you, the Byzantine Empire was around centuries before the advent of electronics let alone walkie talkies; communication was limited. Imagine this attack is planned at night, and the use of torches would

---

[44] Marshall Pease et al., "Reaching Agreement in the Presence of Faults."

alert the opponents. Sending messengers to the other generals might help, but you couldn't be sure they wouldn't get captured. In addition, there's the extra complication of receiving confirmation, but those messengers could also get captured. To make matters worse — and more realistic — what if the opposition sent a saboteur in place of the captured messenger? Same goes for the other generals. Even worse, what if one of the generals was a traitor?[45]

As you can see, this is a seemingly unsolvable problem that has been with humans for most of history. If you take this scenario and transfer it back to Shostak's interactive consistency problem, you have one of the main reasons money wasn't able to be reliably transferred over distance. Without getting too technical, Satoshi Nakamoto's solution to this was to bring Hal Finney's proof-of-work algorithm into Bitcoin's protocol in order to validate and secure consensus. Now we have a reliable distributed ledger, where every node (general) is updated (by the messenger) in regards to the current state of the ledger. Granted, there's a ton more math and code embedded, but for the first time in history the Byzantine Generals Problem was solved.

---

[45] Leslie Lamport et al., "The Byzantine Generals Problem."

Gaining Consensus

*"Words themselves are innocuous;
it is the consensus that gives them true power."*[46]
~ Gloria Naylor

History has been begging for a system that consistently and reliably respects the will of the many. Unfortunately, we haven't been able to avoid our own human nature. Many times, our hubris clouds our judgment. Sometimes, we turn a deaf ear to the lessons of our elders. Oftentimes, we subjugate our will to a smaller, equally fallible set of individuals with their own incentives driving their decisions. Many of us have also given up on taking our own seat at the table. As *Rush* lyricist and drummer Neil Peart once said, "If you choose not to decide, you still have made a choice."

Consensus has not easily been gained. But should it remain that way? Imagine a world in which consensus is easily obtained, undoubtedly reliable, with the rules enforced, and void of human fallibility. It could be easily obtained by allowing every participant equal opportunity to vote in enforcing the rule set. It could be undoubtedly reliable because the rules couldn't be gamed to benefit one individual or group. Imagine the freed-up time and energy if consensus was like this. This consensus protocol would obviate the need for bickering over who controls the rules and how the rules are enforced. What would remain? Harmony and prosperity? Is it too audacious to conceive of an automated Great Plan of Peace?

It is the author's opinion that one of the main reasons we've yet to realize a simple, reliable, and consistent global form of gaining consensus is due primarily to a subset of society's desire for power. People who are inherently power-hungry search for positions of power. This leads to a natural tendency to centralize the decision-making body,

---

[46] Gloria Naylor, "The Meanings of a Word," HERS Column, *The New York Times*.

---

thereby making it easier to set the agenda and get the consensus that benefits them. Therefore, in order to gain this ideal (and more moral) form of consensus, one aspect that we should focus on, as suggested by history, is to decentralize power.

Decentralization

"True progress lies in the direction of decentralization, both territorial and functional, in the development of the spirit of local and personal initiative, and of free federation from the simple to the compound, in lieu of the present hierarchy from the centre to the periphery."[47]

~ Peter Kropotkin

Throughout history, humans have devised many ways to try and be more efficient, automate systems, and reap the rewards of production. Consider for a moment an excerpt from Robert Frost's memorable poem "The Road Not Taken": *"Two roads diverged in a wood, and I — I took the one less traveled by..."*[48] Most of history has attempted to take the path of centralization whereby the decision-making of an organization becomes increasingly concentrated in the hands of a small number of powerful people. While there have been historical benefits to centralization in certain aspects of life, such as improved productivity and increased flexibility or agility, there are also many disadvantages.[49] Some of these are stifled creativity, limited communication, and inflexible decision-making. Many other disadvantages to centralization are difficult to predict second-order effects.

Taking the path of decentralization is the road less taken for a number of reasons. One main reason is that those who seek power must give up power in order to attain true decentralization. Said differently, those individuals who can exercise discipline over their base instincts to control others have the ability to create a decentralized system. Doing so frees up individuals to express themselves creatively. Each

---

[47] Peter Kropotkin, "Anarchism."
[48] Robert Frost, "The Road Not Taken."
[49] Stephen Kowalewski et al., "Boundaries, Scale, and Internal Organization."

---

participant in a decentralized network is also able to provide their personal, experiential inputs into the system, which creates a more robust, informed organization.

Another way to see the benefits of decentralization is to visualize suspension bridges. A suspension bridge is a type of bridge in which the deck is hung below suspension cables on vertical suspenders. Prior to this development, bridges were more subject to collapse due to single points of failure. If one buttress was structurally unsound, the entire bridge could come a tumblin' down. With suspension bridges, the weight and stress is evenly distributed among the cables. Centralized structures have a single point of failure as you'll learn in this chapter.

An even more esoteric way to conceptualize the benefits of decentralization is to view energy following the path of least resistance, which is the physical or metaphorical pathway that provides the least resistance to forward motion by a given object or entity among a set of alternative paths. When water is freed from restriction as in a dam, it's allowed to flow naturally. While a central source can dam up certain water flows for local benefits, the points along the path where nature intended are starved. In this view, centralization is unnatural and potentially destructive despite the propaganda provided by those in the seat of power.

Fall of the Roman Empire

How much land does one emperor need? If you ask early Roman emperors, they'd say "all of it." At one point in the early second century, the Roman Empire controlled almost two million square miles throughout Europe, North Africa, and the Middle East. The Latin phrase *imperium sine fine* ("empire without end") expressed the ideology that neither time nor space limited the Empire. By the late third century, constant disagreements between the eastern and western half of the empire led to a split. With the success of the eastern half and the corruptness of the western half, a separation was necessary. Despite the breakup, there were still many troubles brought on by a small minority attempting to control so much land, resources, and people.

It was difficult for the western empire to defend itself, so its leaders began hiring mercenaries to fight off foreign invasions. This became unsustainable. This might be because someone fighting for a paycheck is less invested compared to someone fighting for a cause. Over time, Barbarian attacks chipped away at the empire. Since the surface area of the Roman Empire was so large, their military defenses were spread thin. It became increasingly difficult for the centralized leaders to coordinate and ward off attacks on all fronts. In the late fourth century, a specific mercenary group called the Goths, who had been assisting the empire in defense, were treated so poorly by the eastern Roman Empire that they revolted against the empire. Despite agreeing to allow the Goths into the empire, it became increasingly difficult to maintain cohesion and a shared sense of identity.[50]

To further complicate things, those close to the source of money were better able to redirect capital and resources to benefit themselves.[51] The Roman peasants were mostly unaware of this as they were not allowed access to the central force. Without local autonomy, individual communities were unable to properly govern themselves. While there were still systems of local governance in place, such as provincial governors and municipal councils, the desire by emperors for increased centralization led to the empire becoming more reliant on the decision-making ability of the few instead of a more sustainable system. As they say, many hands make light work.[52]

Furthermore, Rome was dependent on slaves, which comprised nearly one-third of all Romans. They completed many jobs, which drove the lower class out of the workforce. This led the leaders to provide welfare to the lower class, which further strained the empire's resources. This also further strained the population's connection to the empire; the working class felt increasingly marginalized and detached.

All in all, the fall of the Roman Empire can be seen as a painful lesson in too much hubris. As a star becomes so big it implodes on itself, so too did the Roman Empire. When is enough power and control enough? When is enough resources derived from slave labor enough? When is enough self-importance and legacy enough? The emperors chose to learn these lessons the hard way. What is most unsettling is

---

[50] Ian Garrick-Mason, "Why Rome Fell."

[51] Drew Macmartin, "Hard to Soft Money: The Hyperinflation of the Roman Empire."

[52] Xinyao Zhang. "Centralization and Corruption: The Political Dilemma of the Late Roman Empire."

that the everyday people that lived inside the empire's borders had to feel the effects of the emperors' lessons as well.

<u>Printing Press</u>

Just like people, ideas, and energy want to be free, so too did information. Prior to the fifteenth century, this was hardly the case. The hegemony at the time were the gatekeepers of information. If a European wanted to gain insight into the Bible, they would have to go to the Church where the text was centrally controlled. Back then, writing a book was a difficult task. The average human can write by hand at about four pages per hour. Needless to say, it was painstaking work to copy a book. There were scribes who worked in rooms called scriptoriums inside monasteries where their main job was to copy religious texts.[53] Those that had access to these texts were the monasteries themselves, academic institutions, and the wealthy class. Literacy rates were very low at the time as text was not widespread enough to necessitate the masses being literate.[54]

As the 1430s were coming to a close, Johannes Gutenberg devised a way to take the wooden blocks already used to hand press certain texts and automate the process through a machine now known as the

---

[53] Robert Ayres, *The History and Future of Technology*, 83–86.
[54] Elizabeth Eisenstein, *The Printing Press as an Agent of Change*.

---

printing press. Instead of the human rate of four pages per hour, one could print up to twenty-five pages per hour. The genius of his design was in creating an assembly line for production, which brought down the price for written information over time. But the second-order effect of this technology was what is truly revolutionary.

With the proliferation of all current and potential thought, not just religious thought, knowledge became decentralized. No longer did one need to go to a spiritual or academic leader to learn. No longer was one subject to the morals and preferences of the centralized authority. As mass produced text spread throughout the land, so too did literacy rates. People began to think more for themselves thus becoming less reliant on a central authority.[55]

The freeing of information in print form made way for the Protestant Reformation, the Renaissance period, the scientific Enlightenment, as well as the Industrial Revolution. Thanks to the invention of the printing press, the figurative floodgates of knowledge were opened. The breaking of the informational dam created by centralization set the stage for human flourishing. Decentralization allowed intelligence to flow freely.

---

[55] Eisenstein, *The Printing Press*.

Swiss Confederacy

Starting in 1848, the Swiss began a long streak of relatively peaceful union between many autonomous, independent states known as cantons. Almost two centuries later, Switzerland enjoys much success and prosperity. But it hasn't always been that way.

In the late thirteenth century, the Old Swiss Confederacy was formed when three valley communities united against the counts of Habsburg. Regional cities began to join in order to conquer the areas of what is now Switzerland.[56] By the late fourteenth century, Hamburg was defeated by the now eight cantons. Many wars fought into the early sixteenth century to gain control of the shared land were unsuccessful. By then the confederacy had blossomed to thirteen autonomous cantons.[57]

The Thirty Years' War spanning the early-to-mid-seventeenth century saw some of the most destructive battles Europe has ever seen: Up to eight million soldiers and civilians died. If they didn't die in

---

[56] Clive Church and Randolph Head, *A Concise History of Switzerland*, 20–31.

[57] Oliver Zimmer, *Forging the Swiss Nation*, 50–53.

battle, famine and disease consumed them. During that time, the Swiss Confederacy weathered the storm, having been seen as a "peaceful island." This culminated in the Peace Treaty of Westphalia of 1648 where Europe formally accepted Switzerland as an independent nation.[58] The cantons of the Swiss Confederacy showed that neighbors can help defend one another while still respecting each others' self-sovereignty.

Throughout both World War I and World War II, Switzerland maintained neutrality. They had no desire to fight others' fights. While they were prepared to defend themselves with a strong military strategically nestled in the Alps, each canton rather focused on building the world in which they wanted to live as opposed to forcing their morals on others. They instead created wealth through innovation based on consumer demand above and beyond chocolates and clocks. By allowing each other the space to create value in their own way, inter-canton competition was born, which led to better products thus further benefiting the customers. This creates a virtuous cycle by attracting further investment. Imagine that… not sticking their nose in others' affairs along with creating value that others want led to their development as one of the most prosperous cultures in the world. The Swiss' ability to resist the force of centralization helped make this possible.

One of the biggest centralizing forces currently pushing on Switzerland is the European Union (EU). Formed after World War II, what became the EU started with six countries (Belgium, France, Italy, Luxembourg, the Netherlands, and West Germany). Since then, it has metastasized to twenty-seven countries all of which pay fees in order to give up some level of autonomy. The EU works via overlapping levels of bureaucracy and regulations. Most members use a common fiat currency, the euro, which, since its inception, has lost 85% in

---

[58] Church and Head, *Concise History*, 73–91.

purchasing power compared to gold.[59] This may be due in part to the political instability brought on by attempting to centralize multiple diverse cultures across the union, not to mention the inflationary nature inherent in fiat currencies.

At one point in 1992, the Swiss government actually showed intent to join the EU by first agreeing to join the European Economic Area in order to facilitate a wider trading range. But after multiple referendums were shot down by the citizens, Switzerland showed their respect for direct democracy by backing out. Despite the EU's size, Switzerland has continued to stand for independence, autonomy, and self-sovereignty. Its decentralization is key to maintaining its political and economic stability. The federal government divides power between the now twenty–six cantons. Each canton takes care of its own needs, such as education, healthcare, and social welfare. Due to its direct democratic structure, citizens are able to participate in making decisions through referendums and initiatives, which further decentralizes power. This system also preserves and respects each canton's individual heritage.[60]

It's not hard to see why Switzerland is the only nation from Europe that gets high scores in both fiscal policy and rule of law from the Fraser Institute's "Economic Freedom of the World" index.[61] Could prosperity be as simple as resisting the power-hungry's desire for centralization, helping each other in defense of private property, and focusing on providing services to neighbors? If the history of the Swiss Confederacy has anything to say about this, then the answer is emphatically yes.

---

[59] Jan Nieuwenhuijs, "Since Its Inception, the Euro Has Devalued by 85% Against Gold."
[60] Aubrey Diem et al., "Switzerland: Government and Society."
[61] Daniel Mitchell, "The Secret of Swiss Success Is Decentralization.";
Gwartney et al., *Economic Freedom of the World 2022.*

Fall of the Soviet Union

Prior to the creation of one of the most centralized economies in history, Russia's way of life was based off of feudalism, whereby the Tsar king would rule his large land holdings by reaping the productivity gains from their peasant serfs. The Tsar at the time was reluctant to give in to industrialization in fear that it would lead to a decrease in his power. The unfortunate trade-off for this was stagnant economic growth, which put Russia behind much of the developing west.[62] Couple that with an impoverished working class clamoring for freedom, and you got yourselves the makings of an uprising. The centralizing forces of centuries of authoritarian monarchy eventually led to its foundational breakdown.[63] But that's not the funny part yet...

Beginning with the German invasion during World War I, the throne that had lasted for three hundred years was, well, overthrown. The replacement government was headed by the communist Bolshevik leader, Vladimir Lenin, who brought Marxist ideology to what became known as the United Socialist Soviet of Russia (USSR) in 1917.

---

[62] Thomas Owen, "The Russian Industrial Society."
[63] Robert Service, *The Last of the Tsars.*

Basically, these Marxists wanted a classless society whereby there was no private property and everyone worked for the common good... everyone except the centralized ruling class, that is. But they were the good guys; socialists who were more fair and equal, so it's okay, right? Wait, what's to stop them from becoming dictators in a centralized system like this? [insert cricket noises] Let's digress.

Early in Lenin's Communist Party of the Soviet Union, they did fun stuff like kicking out anyone who disagreed with them and implemented their extractive brand of socialism where the authority centralizes wealth and resources by extracting it via the working class. Unsurprisingly, a civil war broke out within a year. The government then nationalized all industries and effectively seized control of the entire economy. Due to the effects of excessive centralization, the economy imploded. In a "things can't get any better, right?" kind of moment, Lenin died of a stroke in 1924 and was succeeded by Josef Stalin.

In 1928, Stalin implemented his five-year plan, which further nationalized all the industries to an even greater level of micromanagement. Every farm, factory, and store was controlled from their ivory towers. All prices and economic activities were set by Stalin's government. An increased focus on industrialization and the building of military power were prioritized. The inefficiencies of the rural Soviet agricultural sector, which composed the majority of the Russian population, led Stalin to force farmers to work for state-directed communal farms. The majority of all agricultural resources were redirected to feed the industrial behemoth located at the center of the economy. This extractive governmental overreach was known as collectivization, which ultimately led to the death of tens of millions Russians.[64]

Despite the short-term success of economic growth in Stalin's first five years, the system was becoming less sustainable. One unintended

---

[64] Anne Applebaum, *Red Famine*, ch. 4, 13; Timothy Snyder, *Bloodlands: Europe Between Hitler and Stalin.*

consequence of centralization was the blatant disregard for the workers' motivation. Imagine that, the more controlling someone is in a relationship, the less connected and respected the other feels. Why work harder to create more widgets when you've already filled your quota? This disconnect from personal incentives showed itself in low worker productivity.[65]

One of the biggest issues with this planned economy was the lack of accurate and abundant information. Unnecessary and outdated industries remained. Innovation stagnated due to the limited amount of thoughts and perspectives available in the inner circle of power.[66] Eventually, the centrally planned socialist experiment collapsed under its own weight. As the collapse happened, the tyrannical impulses of Stalin showed themselves. Due to the centralized structure, there were no checks in place to counter him. Regardless of Gorbechov's perestroika, the attempt of restructuring the economics and politics, the damage was done.

---

[65] Robert Allen, "The Rise and Decline of the Soviet Economy," pp. 860–63.
[66] Chi Ling Chan, "Fallen Behind."

Internet

In the late 1960s, researchers and scientists needed a reliable way to share information over long distances. Their solution was to create a distributed model of connected computers known technically as a "packet switched network." Funded by the Advanced Research Projects Agency (ARPA) of the United States Department of Defense, ARPANET was formed. One benefit of this model was if one computer were to go down, the information could still be reliably shared between the other computers on the network as opposed to being controlled by a central authority. At the time though, there were only a handful of computers on the network.[67]

As time went on, more and more networks began popping up around the world. Each of them ran on their own set of code. Basically, these networks didn't speak the same language. For these technologies to scale, there would have to be further systems put in place for interoperability. In the early 1970s, the first iteration of the Transmission Control Protocol was created. By creating an open

---

[67] Katie Hafner, *Where Wizards Stay Up Late*.

protocol that all networks could utilize and coordinate activity, decentralization of information was further proliferated as entities did not have to rely on centralized, proprietary entities to ensure proper delivery of information packets. By the early 1980s, Transmission Control Protocol/Internet Protocol (TCP/IP) was adopted as the standard, which obsoleted the need for ARPANET.[68]

Further developments throughout the 1980s and 1990s allowed for this decentralized information sharing to flow freely across the world. Eventually this opened up to the widespread commercial use that many of us take for granted today. While many companies successfully attempted to centralize and monetize their data via walled gardens and data silos, the internet's ability to allow peer-to-peer networking further promoted decentralization. These networks allowed individual users to directly share information with each other, instead of going through centralized servers or data centers.[69]

The internet has opened up the world to decentralized collaboration, empowered individuals, and negated much of the need for third-party authorities to manage information sharing. Access to the internet, which started out as researchers and scientists sharing information over long distances, has now become what the United Nations declared in 2016, "a basic human right."

---

[68] Barry Leiner et al., "Brief History of the Internet," 4–7.
[69] Francesca Musiani, "Giants, Dwarfs and Decentralized Alternatives."

Decentralization

"Centralization as a system is inconsistent with a non-violent structure of society." [70]
~ Mahatma Gandhi

History has repeatedly yearned for the implementation of systems that utilize some form of decentralization. Powerful people have had to deal with the repercussions of their greed and desire to centralize power and authority. Equally, there have been some that have countered this primitive desire with inventions that unlock humanity's ability to coordinate action free of top-down rule.

While there are benefits to centralization in certain aspects of life, there is one glaring weakness: that of coercion. As the examples of the Roman Empire and Soviet Russia have shown, centralization required both force by the centralizing entity and a disregard for those without a voice inside said system. Our current political system unfortunately seems to promote further centralization in that each party grabs for ever more power. Each time the political pendulum swings to the other party, they inherit that level of power in addition to attempting to garner more. This results in an increasingly centralized, coercive system.

Decentralized protocols promote voluntary action between participants. When authority is more evenly distributed, the effect of coercion is diminished. If we want to ascend to Gandhi's vision of a "non-violent structure of society," we must appreciate and embrace decentralization.

---

[70] Mahatma Gandhi, *All Men Are Brothers*, 124.

Trust Minimization

"Fool me once, shame on... shame on you.
Fool me... you can't get fooled again."[71]
~ George W Bush

Confidence, faith, assurance, reliance. These are just some of the thoughts and feelings one has in a relationship built upon trust. As we all have learned at some point in our lives, trust takes time and effort to build but can swiftly be broken. Some of us have been on both sides, and anyone who's been around long enough to experience broken trust knows that the relationship has irrevocably changed.

We all have the ability to be gullible. We also all have the ability to deceive. With the ever-increasing amount of information that we deal with in our daily lives, it's easy to let things slip past us. History is rife with examples of us trusting the wrong person, group, organization, or government. What we should learn from these episodes is not to be less trusting. Rather, we should embrace protocols that minimize the need for trust. To gain a sense of how trust is easily broken and also how trustless systems can benefit us, please read on...

---

[71] Quoted in Geoff Tibballs, *I Wish I Hadn't Said That*. Available via YouTube: https://youtu.be/JhmdEq3JhoY?t=111 (1:51–2:07).

Victor Lustig

Victor Lustig was born in 1890 into an aristocratic family in what is now the Czech Republic. Or… Victor Lustig was born in 1890 as the son of Ludwig Lustig, the mayor of Hostinne. Or… Victor Lustig was born in 1890 under the name Robert Miller to a poor peasant family in Bohemia. Or… Victor Lustig, regardless of what story he told, was born a con man through and through.

Lustig grew up honing his scamming skills. By his late teens, he had moved past pickpocketing and burglary on his way to becoming a top card shark hustling in the streets of Paris. During this time, Lustig began to develop his persona: He became fluent in many languages, wore tailored suits, and gave himself the title of Count based on an erroneous story about being a nobleman from the former Bohemian kingdom. His proper and precise mannerisms made it difficult for the layperson to properly judge his character.

As Lustig settled in North America, he perfected his craft through scams like the Rumanian box where he claimed to print magic money (aka, counterfeiting) then sell the contraption to unsuspecting victims.

Lustig's sleight of hand skill was so deft he was able to swindle a Missouri bank out of Liberty Bonds, cash, and the deed to farmland.[72]

But Lustig's greatest accomplishment came when he returned to Paris in the mid-1920s to sell something that was not his to sell: the Eiffel Tower. At the time, the Eiffel Tower was in need of repair, and the cost of maintenance was rather expensive. Since the original government plan was to tear it down in 1909, Lustig decided to bring together the largest scrap metal dealers in Paris to bid for the job of demolishing the tower. Acting as a government employee, Lustig chose his mark. He set his sights on the smallest of the scrap metal dealers, André Poisson. Not only was he able to sell the Eiffel Tower, he also was able to get Poisson to offer a bribe for preferential treatment. Despite being scammed, Poisson did not report it as he was most likely embarrassed and did not want to be publicly ridiculed.[73]

After waiting for things to settle, Victor Lustig returned to Paris to... you guessed it... sell the Eiffel Tower *again*. Unfortunately for Lustig, one of the new scrap metal dealers was suspicious and immediately reported him to authorities. After escaping to the United States, Lustig attempted con after con. At one point he conned Al Capone out of money by getting Capone to loan him $50,000 for a hot stock tip. He put the money in the bank, waited, then told Capone he lost the money but would pay him out of his own pocket, which was Capone's original $50,000. Capone, appreciating Lustig's honesty, gave him a handsome reward for the troubles, which was the intended result of the con.

After attempting to counterfeit nearly one million dollars, Lustig gained the attention of the Secret Service. A swift investigation led to his arrest, but this didn't stop him. In 1935, he escaped from jail by tying stolen bedsheets together and climbed down to reclaim his freedom. This didn't last long. Within a month, Lustig was captured

---

[72] Christopher Sandford, *The Man Who Conned the World*, ch. 2, 7.
[73] Sandford, *Conned the World*, ch. 5.

once again, placed in Alcatraz, and eventually died of pneumonia in 1947.

Was Victor Lustig a good person? Absolutely not. But he did understand a few critical things about human nature. He knew people were inherently trusting. He knew the holes in the social fabric through which he could weave his lies. Had there been systems in place for his marks to check the validity of his statements, many would not have fallen for such deceit.

The Federal Reserve

As opportunistic people usually do, they never let a good crisis go to waste. That's exactly what six rich men did in 1910. On the heels of the 1907 Bankers' Panic, where major stock markets crumbled, bank runs were as common as bankruptcies, and the economy was in recession, a group of executive bankers were brought together by then Senate Republican leader, Nelson Aldrich in a secret meeting to discuss a way to fix the perceived errors in the way banking was conducted. This meeting was not only kept secret from the public but also the government.[74] What a way to build societal trust, eh?

This clandestine vacay to now famous Jekyll Island, Georgia, led to the creation of the Federal Reserve, a monopolistic central bank, which utilizes a system known as fractional reserve banking. Fractional reserve banking is a system where banks are not required to hold 100% of your money available for withdrawal. They do this in order to allow commercial banks to create money. The banks then loan out more than they have in reserve. The idea is that by allowing banks to only hold a

---

[74] Roger Lowenstein, *America's Bank*; Jacob Goldstein, *The True Story of a Made-Up Thing*, 133–34.

fraction of deposits, the resulting borrowing and spending helps spur economic growth.

The funny thing is the Federal Reserve is neither federal (it is an entity independent of the government) nor does it have any reserves, beyond the digital base money it itself creates. As American economist and banker Marriner Stoddard Eccles said, "If there were no debts in our money system, there wouldn't be any money."[75] While it is debatable that economic growth stems from money printing, it is also debatable that a fractionalized monetary system leads to booms and busts as well as a perpetual state of inflation as more dollars in circulation are needed to keep the system from collapsing in on itself. Despite the end result finally being approved by Congress and Woodrow Wilson, the average American didn't have a say in the decision... outside of who they voted in as a proxy. While this is common practice in developed governments, changing the entire monetary system, it doesn't do much for the everyday citizen's trust in their institutions.[76]

By 1913, the Federal Reserve Act was enacted by Congress. This allowed for the creation of a centrally controlled banking system, which regulates monetary policy and manages the money supply. From this came twelve regional Federal Reserve Banks and a Board of Governors. The Federal Reserve now has the power to lend money to banks, regulate interest rates, and act as a lender of last resort.[77]

Not to understate this, but that's a lot of power. The value of our time and labor was arbitrarily determined. They literally rewrote the book on how value is owned, transacted, and, most importantly, priced. And we, the average citizen, are expected to trust in a system in which we were not trusted with courtesy to agree, disagree, provide input, or even know about its creation. How's that for trustworthiness?

---

[75] Marriner Eccles, Testimony Before Congress, April 5, 1943, 111.
[76] Edward Griffin, *The Creature From Jekyll Island.*
[77] John Wood, *A History of Central Banking*, 162–170.

Now, we have a debt-based monetary system, which means it is literally based on the trust that debts will be repaid. But if banks are required to hold even a fraction of depositor funds in reserve, and those loans are based on the trust that the subsequent loans will be paid, how can one trust that the funds they purport to own will be returned to them if more than a few depositors are in need? And what's to say the value of the nominal amount being repaid is anywhere close to the real value when considering the effect of inflation?

Charles Ponzi

Similar to the aforementioned fractionalized banking system, Charles Ponzi made a name for himself by gaining the trust of his depositors only to fleece them of their hard-earned wealth. Charles was born in Italy in 1882 to a formerly wealthy family. With what funds they had left, his parents sent him to the University of Rome. Ponzi flourished, but not in the academic sense. He consistently skipped classes instead opting for the party lifestyle. After four unsuccessful years, Charles left school with nothing to show for it.

In 1903, Charles Ponzi left for the hope of greater opportunities found in America. He arrived in Boston, Massachusetts, with $2.50 to his name. For his first four years in America, Charles worked odd jobs just to keep food on the table.[78] This forced him to frequently move about the east coast until he settled in Montreal, Canada, where he received a job opportunity as a clerk in a local bank. After the bank went under due to poor money management, Ponzi resorted to a life of crime. He spent three years in prison for forgery. After his release, he

---

[78] Mary Darby, "In Ponzi We Trust."

moved to Atlanta and was sentenced shortly after to two more years for smuggling Italian immigrants. After his second release, Ponzi spent the next five years working odd jobs all up and down the southwestern United States.

Settling back in Boston in the late 1910s, Ponzi fell upon an opportunity to be a commodities broker. His first trade was a doozy as he attempted to sell someone else's cheese. Yes, you heard that right. Ponzi literally sold 5,387 pounds of cheese that wasn't his. After another failed attempt at business, this time in advertising, Ponzi stumbled into a rare arbitrage opportunity. Arbitrage is the practice of taking advantage of a difference in prices in two or more markets. He ended up receiving an advertising request from a Spanish company. Inside was a voucher for postage stamps. This was known as an International Reply Coupon, or IRC for short. He noticed the arbitrage opportunity in the difference of exchange rates between the foreign vouchers and the local postage. None of this IRC arbitrage opportunity was illegal, and Charles profited greatly from it.[79]

In 1920 Ponzi used his new-found wealth to create the Securities Exchange Company (not to be confused with the governmental Securities Exchange Commission). His business model was to sell stock advertising 50% interest in 90 days. He used the success from his IRC windfalls to get investors to trust that their funds were used to buy IRCs. But in reality, funds from new investors were used to pay off old investors. Charles Ponzi made $8.5M in the first half of 1920. Even though the US Postal Union suspended the sale of IRCs, Ponzi was able to keep the scheme going by telling people he ran an IRC network in Europe.[80]

Later that year, the US Post Office changed the IRC exchange rate. Due to his increasing net worth, the Boston Globe began to investigate his business practices, which prompted Ponzi to decline new investments. Even though he was able to pay out upwards of $1M,

---

[79] Mitchell Zuckoff, *Ponzi's Scheme*, 86–97.
[80] Darby, "In Ponzi We Trust."

investors' trust grew thin. Similar to a bank run, investors began to file claims. Thanks to the fortunate investors who were made whole, around 20,000 victims were able to recoup nearly 40% of their original investment. The thousands of investors who were not as fortunate received nothing.

Convicted of federal mail fraud charges, he received a five-year prison sentence, which ultimately got reduced by one year for good behavior. State prosecutors were able to add charges that earned Ponzi another seven to nine years. After making bail, Ponzi escaped to Florida to concoct another scheme, this time in the real estate market. 200% return in 60 days. Florida authorities shut it down earning Ponzi another year in prison for violating state securities law.[81]

Having been fluent in Italian, Ponzi secured a job in the kitchen and restaurant of an Italian freighter under the name Andrea Luciana. To try and end the manhunt, he faked suicide by asking friends to put a suicide note and some of his clothes on a Florida beach. Thinking he avoided law enforcement, Ponzi, trusting a complete stranger, shared his original identity with a shipmate who immediately turned him in. He was arrested in New Orleans and shipped back to Massachusetts where he spent seven years.[82]

Having never obtained proper US citizenship, Ponzi was deported back to Italy. Not being able to hold down a job, he traveled to Brazil to find work. A quick decline in health led to his death. His net worth at the time was $75.[83] His namesake is now in the popular lexicon. A Ponzi Scheme is described as a form of fraud that lures investors and pays profits to earlier investors with funds from more recent investors.

---

[81] Zuckoff, *Ponzi's Scheme*, 302.
[82] Donald Dunn, *Ponzi: The Incredible True Story*, 341–42.
[83] Darby, "In Ponzi We Trust."

Navajo Code Talkers

For a time during World War II, it was looking like the Axis powers of Germany, Japan, and Italy were going to dominate. Axis successes like Pearl Harbor were becoming more common. It was as if the Axis were always one step ahead of the Allies. Communication during war is and always was a double-edged sword; if the message got intercepted, battles — not to mention lives — could be lost. Code cracking was extremely important to each side's success, and many resources were exhausted in order to gain even the slightest tactical advantage. Famed computer scientist Alan Turing's efforts were crucial in cracking Nazi codes during the war. The search for new ways to minimize trust during communication was always on the forefront of the minds of military leaders.[84]

Native American languages were successfully used to encode messages in previous wars although the codes had since been broken. Even though it was proposed to use the Navajo language as code at the beginning of World War II, it wasn't until after Pearl Harbor that this

---

[84] Andrew Hodges, *Alan Turing: The Enigma*.

option was explored. The mounting losses spurred the Marine Corps to jump at the opportunity. They did so by simulating combat situations with Navajo men who were able to encode and decode three-line messages in twenty seconds. This was a drastic improvement from the previous standard of thirty minutes. The Marines then took to recruiting up to two-hundred Navajo men. That lofty goal was later parsed down to one platoon of twenty-nine individuals. In 1942, these Navajo men were sworn into Platoon 382 and ordered to begin writing their code.[85]

What made the Navajo language difficult to decipher was that it was not a written language; it was communicated orally, and the language had no structural alphabet. This made it nearly impossible to translate. To further strengthen the code, the military added code substitutions. For example, different vehicles were substituted with Navajo words for different animals (dive bombers were "chicken hawks" and battleships were "whales"). What started with 211 vocabulary code words grew to 411 throughout the war's course.[86] Further encryption was added when the Navajo assigned a word to each of the letters in the English alphabet. To add another layer of security, many different words were paired to the common letters of the English alphabet.[87] There's an entire Navajo Code Talker Dictionary if you're interested in further study.[88]

Navajo Code Talkers were absolutely critical to the success of the Marine Corps in the Pacific theater during World War II. Their efficiency and effectiveness saved countless lives as well as limit the United States' time spent engaged in war in the Pacific. One officer, Major Connor, spoke highly of the Navajo platoon when he stated, "Were it not for the Navajos, the Marines would never have taken Iwo Jima."[89] Their skill and courage earned them many accolades including

---

[85] Chester Nez and Judith Avila, *Code Talker.*

[86] Deanne Durrett, *Unsung Heroes of World War II.*

[87] Adam Jevec, "'Semper Fidelis, Code Talkers'."

[88] Naval History and Heritage Command, "Navajo Code Talkers' Dictionary."

[89] Durrett, *Unsung Heroes*, 92.

the Congressional Gold Medal. By creating extremely secure and secret communications during World War II, the Navajo Code Talkers exemplified the benefits of trust minimization.

Gold Codes

Some of us are lucky enough to entrust the keys to our hearts to someone special. What about the keys to global nuclear annihilation? Would you trust one person with that much power? Didn't think so. It is for this reason that the United States government invented a trust-minimized system for the handling and execution of the keys to outright nuclear war known as Gold Codes. Leading up to the Cuban Missile Crisis of 1962, President Kennedy thought it would be prudent to be prepared in case of an imminent strike. At that time, it seemed like either side could strike on any given day. The solution was known as the "nuclear football," a large, black suitcase capable of accessing not only the weapons but also the top military officials and his Chief of Staff from any location on the globe. Each person with access needed the ability to verify their identity. That's where the codes, also known as "the biscuit," came in.[90]

Because the president of the United States is commander-in-chief of the armed forces, the launch codes for the country's nuclear weapons are entrusted to this human. Obviously, it would be unwise to give

---

[90] Ron Rosenbaum, *How the End Begins*, 32–36.

anyone unilateral control over the fate of humanity. We're all fallible, and even if the person occupying the presidency were benevolent, they could easily misplace things like their car keys, smartphone, or even, say, the Gold Codes of weapons of mass destruction, right? Don't think that's possible? Former President Bill Clinton allegedly did misplace the biscuit, which went missing for months.[91] An assaination attempt on Ronald Regan led to the Gold Codes being left in the hospital hallway for hours after staff removed his clothes while attempting to save his life. Richard Nixon drove off without his codes once. Jimmy Carter even once left the biscuit in his dry cleaning.[92]

It is for such reasons that there are actually as many as five or six nuclear footballs; one that travels with the president, one with the vice president, one that remains at the White House, and others assigned to other high ranking officials. Inside the suitcase is an aluminum briefcase containing communication equipment as well as documents containing launch options. Prior to any launch, proper identity verification via each member's biscuit is mandatory. The verification would simply be two words shared by one and two words by another. For example, "golf-mike" must be followed by "foxtrot-yankee" for proper verification. Once these highly classified codes have been verified, the strike sequence can commence. The President would also discuss possible alternative strategies with his Chief of Staff. Encrypted orders are then sent to the Pentagon where they are decrypted and compared to similar coded orders stored safely at their facility. Once those codes are verified, they are sent to the launch site where five, remote, high-ranking individuals must vote on firing the missiles. Each has a key that they must turn simultaneously in order to fire the

---

[91] Andrew Naughtie, "Did Bill Clinton Really 'Lose' the Nuclear Codes as Trump Claimed — and Does it Matter?"
[92] John Donvan, "President Bill Clinton Lost Nuclear Codes While in Office, New Book Claims."; Ryan Pickrell, "Trump's Erratic Presidency."

missiles. Even then, officers can veto the strike if they do not believe it is legal or if it is fraudulent.[93]

While the protocol may be different depending on location (submarines for example), multiple layers of verification are in place in order to minimize the trust in the system. This is obviously necessary to avoid all-out hell on Earth. There's a need to know the authenticity of order. There's a need to know the order is not based on the whims of a single megalomaniac. In situations like these, there's a need to minimize trust.

---

[93] Danielle McNally, "These Women Are the Last Thing Standing Between You and Nuclear War."

Trust Minimization

"Trust, but verify."
~ Ronald Reagan[94]

History has shown time and again humans trusting others only to have that trust broken. The current systems in place necessitate the need for trust. Due to the nature of the fractional reserve system, we must trust the money "in the bank" will actually be there when we need it. We must trust the class of people connected to the money spigot will behave morally. We must trust that a few unelected bureaucrats are making educated decisions free of personal conflicts of interests.

But what if a system came along that negated the need for trust? What if the simple answer was in applying technological innovation that utilized verification over trust? What if there were already a system in place that is based on trust minimization? What if history has been clamoring for such an innovation? What if it's been right under our noses for over a decade now?

That being said, human nature won't automatically evolve to a point where everyone is trustworthy. Instead of wasting our energy hoping this were different or will change, we should instead accept it and move forward with empathy. Trustless systems like Bitcoin acknowledge the fallibility of humans. It does so by obsoleting the need for trusted third parties. This trust minimization allows for fair settlement of value between peers. All transactions and funds can easily be verified by any and every network participant. By running a node, you can guarantee the issuance schedule, the total supply, and the underlying and unchangeable code.

---

[94] Quoted in Barton Swaim, "'Trust, But Verify', An Untrustworthy Political Phrase."

Censorship Resistance

"Censorship reflects a society's lack of confidence in itself."[95]
~ Potter Stewart

Tools can equally help and hurt. Think of a hammer. It can make a family's dinner table. It can help build shelter from the elements. It has helped shape humanity for the better in countless ways. It can also be used as a weapon. Just because we can hurt each other with hammers, does that mean that hammers should be outlawed? Obviously not. The same logic holds true for censorship.

While there are certain things that most agree should not be a part of civilized society, giving carte blanche to a few decision-makers to determine what is or isn't appropriate is a recipe for ruin. It leads to an uneven playing field; those in power tend to wield censorship as a weapon as opposed to a tool. Throughout history, society, usually counterculture, has invented ways to be resistant to censorship.

One of the most effective forms of censorship is the choice to ignore; when we leave the act of censorship to the individual, it removes the unintended consequences brought forth by the broad-brush of top-down institutions while still allowing the collective to express itself from the bottom up. Let's listen to the examples and non-examples of censorship history has shared.

---

[95] Justice Stewart, *"Ginzburg v. United States."*

The Death of Socrates

    In 399 BCE, an elderly man at the ripe age of 71 represented a clear and present danger to the current establishment... because of his thoughts. The leaders at the time claimed Socrates was spewing unholy disrespect by speaking negatively about the Greek gods, which was, in their view, corrupting the minds of the Athenian youth. Some believe these charges were a cover for a deeper political struggle.[96] This stemmed from two of Socrates' former students rising to power during the ongoing Peloponnesian War. These tyrants stood for the pro-Spartan oligarchy, killed supporters of democracy, and confiscated private property from their own Athenian citizens. They were concerned being ostensibly tied to their former teacher, they might be seen as enemies of the state by association. Whether these charges against Socrates were motivated by politics or religion though is still up for debate by scholars.[97]

---

[96] Doug Linder, "The Trial of Socrates."
[97] Gregory McBrayer "Corrupting the Youth."

Regardless of the baseless nature of the charges, Socrates was considered to have been fomenting insurrection; attempting to form a counterrevolution against the Spartan-led Athenian government. Socrates was enlightening the young men of Athens to rise up against tyranny. Socrates' war crimes led to his trial in 399 BCE in which he was sentenced to death. Interestingly, the Athenian government did not truly want to kill him; they wanted to scare him enough to leave Athens. In addition to the option of leaving Athens, Socrates could have renounced his pro-democratic stance, stopped expressing contempt for the current government and court, or have received a moderate fine of which he could have reasonably chosen the amount.[98] Not a bad deal, right?

Instead, Socrates declined all options because doing so would be admitting guilt. Running away, as some infer, would have set a bad example of being a model citizen. The funny thing is, Socrates was neither pro-democratic nor pro-oligarchy, depending on who's version of history you choose to believe. He was attempting to uphold his philosophical principles.[99] He believed in an ideal society that would be governed by wise and knowledgeable individuals, regardless of social status or wealth. Socrates' moral compass was so in tune he chose to rather stay and accept punishment. That punishment was to drink hemlock tea, which was made from a highly poisonous plant capable of inducing death.[100]

The real threat of Socrates was his ability to rationally question the dogmatism of unchecked authority. As stated in Plato's *Apology*, Socrates said to the court, "I am better off than he is—for he knows nothing, and thinks that he knows. I neither know nor think that I know."[101] Socrates' self-awareness of his ignorance was what made him truly wise. This wisdom was the foundation for his humility, which

---

[98] Richard Kraut, *Socrates and the State*, 16–18.
[99] Kraut, *Socrates and the State*, 51–53.
[100] Emily Wilson, *The Death of Socrates*, 5–8.
[101] Plato, "The Apology of Socrates," 21d.

permitted Socrates to ask challenging questions, even when directed at authority. Socrates spoke directly to authority when he said "...if I say again that the greatest good of man is daily to converse about virtue [aretē], and all that concerning which you hear me examining myself and others, and that the life which is unexamined is not worth living."[102] Socrates was more concerned with avoiding unrighteousness than avoiding death.[103]

He attacked the morality of the court by saying "for if you think that by killing men you can avoid the accuser censoring your lives, you are mistaken; that is not a way of escape which is either possible or honorable; the easiest and noblest [kalos] way is not to be crushing others, but to be improving yourselves."[104] This depth of consciousness bruised the egos of the court. Unfortunately, the power of the unchecked authority won out despite Socrates' logic.

History has since echoed Socrates' logic. In *A Clash of Kings*, George R. R. Martin has Tyrion say, "When you tear out a man's tongue, you are not proving him a liar, you're only telling the world that you fear what he might say."[105] Censorship does little to propel society forward; rather, it stagnates. Those that wield the tool of censorship the most are the ones that stall societal discourse the most. The irony of this story is that, despite the best efforts of the governing body to cancel him, Socrates' essence, his love of wisdom, is what stood the test of time.

---

[102] Plato, "The Apology of Socrates," 38a.
[103] Kraut, *Socrates and the State*.
[104] Plato, "The Apology of Socrates," 39d.
[105] George Martin, *A Clash of Kings*, 199.

Samizdat

Faced with massive censorship stemming from the post-Stalin Soviet state, Russian citizens needed a means of self-expression and free speech. In the late 1960s, censorship of Soviet citizens was enforced whenever the ruling class felt their ideology was being threatened by alternative religious, political, or sexual views. The Communist party had several organizations tasked with controlling the thoughts of their constituents. For example, Goskomizdat was the committee in charge of censoring all printed materials from the apparently abhorrent *Chronicles of Narnia* to angsty teenage poetry. While the Goskino committee was in charge of regulating cinema, the Gosteleradio was in charge of overseeing radio and television broadcasts… to keep the dangerous jazz musicians at bay.[106]

Enter Samizdat, which constituted an underground patchwork of individuals spread wide across East and Central Europe with the intent to peacefully protest the Stalinistic suppression of self-expression through the creation of self-published media. The literal meaning of the

---

[106] Ilya Kiriya and Elena Sherstoboeva, "Russian Media Piracy," 842.

word Samizdat is in fact "self publishing" ("sam" being self and "izdat" being publish). The creation of publications was a slow and arduous task. One could not go into a library to use or borrow a typewriter without first providing their name and ID. If someone were caught using it for any non-state sponsored media, they could be at risk of being sent to prison or even a psychiatric facility.[107]

The process of writing was rather difficult. Most of the printed material was done by hand on thin pieces of "onion paper," which are similar to that of carbon copy paper. The ink was made in a washing machine containing moss and burned tires. The transporting of these documents was a highly risky endeavor. The brave souls had to hide papers inside hidden pockets in their clothes to transport at the risk of up to three years of prison... for words... that somebody else didn't like.[108]

Through an underground matrix of people standing for freedom of speech, creative production techniques, a culture of embracing anonymity, valuing intellectual progress over personal accolades, and a respect for human rights — not to mention the implementation of a decentralized network — the Samizdat were able to overcome the control one of the most domineering governing body in history. In 1988, the Soviet security agency, the KGB, released a report illuminating the extent of their censorship. Committee Chairman Chebrikov ended the report stating "The KGB is implementing measures to prevent and suppress in a timely fashion negative incidents connected with the distribution of anonymous materials of hostile content and to increase the effectiveness of the effort to identify the authors and distributors of these materials."[109] This brought an end to censorship by the Communists and allowed free-flowing expression once again to the people of the land. Ideas had the freedom to be judged by the quality of their thought as opposed to the views of the elite.

---

[107] Gordon Skilling, *Samizdat*, 4–6, ch. 2.
[108] Ann Komaromi, "Samizdat and Soviet Dissident Publics," 78.
[109] Library of Congress, "Revelations from the Russian Archives."

Similar to how a stream will eventually find its way around a dam, the Samizdat movement was able to circumvent the bureaucratic, socialist micromanagement of natural, human self-expression.

The overbearingness of groupthink at that time in history should be a warning sign for current and future generations. The history of the Samizdat shows that the spirit of human ingenuity can outlast the desire of totalitarian control. As Russian-born British human rights activist and Samizdat self-publisher Vladimir Bukovsky once said "Power rests on nothing other than people's consent to submit."[110] Those who choose to be submissive are the ones that give others the power to censor. It is our responsibility then to peacefully protest and resist the force of censorship.

---

[110] Vladimir Bukovsky, "To Build a Castle," 191.

Great Firewall of China

You likely learned about the Great Wall of China sometime around middle school. You remember, the series of forts connected by a wall spanning thousands of feet along the northern border of China? It was created as a buttress to stifle the advance of enemy armies from the north. The purpose of the wall was to keep unwanted things out, and it did so extremely well throughout history. So it's logically consistent that the Chinese would fall back on their heritage by creating another great wall. This time, instead of attacking armies, the communist Chinese government was trying to contain the flow of information to their unlawful citizens (but also the lawful ones too). Just like the original wall, the Great Firewall of China was created brick by brick; the Great Firewall was not implemented during the passing of a single, comprehensive regulation. Many laws, regulations, and technical restrictions have been put in place over the years.

The first brick in the wall was called "Regulations for the Management of Computer Information Networks" in 1997.[111] It aimed to require Internet Service Providers (ISPs) to register with the government in order to monitor and censor any material deemed a threat to national security. ISPs were censored from sharing any information that the Communist party would deem harmful to social order, public safety, or national security. The important point here is "...information that the *Communist party* would deem harmful..." It's like if the player of a game is also acting as referee. Not surprisingly, fines and criminal prosecution were doled out for those who did not comply.

Another brick in the wall came in 2000 and was titled "Measures for the Administration of Internet Information Services," which in part created a licensing system for Internet information services.[112] It was forbidden for anyone to be found using the internet without a license. The government essentially gave themselves the control to monitor online activity, restrict access to certain websites, censor content, and collect user data. Records were kept for ninety days in order to search through colossal amounts of data for possible infractions stemming from a laundry list of no-no's. Fines of between 5,000 and 50,000 yuan (~$7,250) were likely for those who did not comply.

Further laws such as the "Provisions on the Administration of Internet News Information Services" followed in 2005. These regulations focused on labeling and tracking anyone who facilitated the spreading of newsworthy information on the internet. All western social media platforms (Facebook, Twitter, Google, YouTube, etc) were banned.[113] Wouldn't it be nice to have a complete history of anyone who disagreed with you including their place of residence,

---

[111] State Council, "Regulations for the Protection and Management of the International Networking of Computer Information Networks."

[112] Rogier Creemers, "Internet Information Service Management Measures."

[113] Ministry of Information Industry, "Regulations on the Administration of Internet News Information Services."

personal information, and their entire search history? China thinks so. By this point, the bricks in the wall were becoming formidable.

In addition to the mounting regulations, the Communist apparatus also added technical guardrails for enhanced control over internet access. DNS filtering was implemented, which is a security technique used to stop Internet users from accessing unapproved websites on a server. IP blocking helped officials block requests from specific IP (Internet Protocol) addresses. Keyword filtering helped the powerful with blocking emails based on keywords in the emails of the powerless.[114] In 2011, WeChat was created as a convenient way for Chinese citizens to conduct much of their online life. The WeChat app includes messaging, social media, money transferring, maps, games, and much more. This might be considered a win for the Chinese citizens until the realization sets in that it is essentially one big honeypot, which gives the government even more unbridled surveillance and control.

In the recent annual report, "Freedom in the World 2023," human rights organization, Freedom House, gave China an Internet freedom score of 10 out of 100, which ranks them dead last out of all sixty-five countries assessed.[115] The report highlighted the immense amount of human capital wasted in order to limit others' freedom of access to information. It said, "The country's network of some 20 million pro-CCP volunteer internet commentators and more than 2 million paid employees continued to aggressively monitor and censor online communications."[116] Imagine the innovation that amount of collective brainpower could create for current and future generations. Instead, the Chinese choose to hire more ranchers to quell their cattle's desire for the grass-fed pastures of cognitive diversity. It's been said that ingenuity creates and totalitarianism consumes. That sucking sound

---

[114] Internet Society, "Internet Society Perspectives on Internet Content Blocking: An Overview."
[115] Freedom House, "Freedom in the World 2023."
[116] Freedom House, "Freedom in the World 2023: China."

you hear... it's the consumption of the Chinese people's creative capacity being converted into censorship and control.

Arab Spring

In 2010, a Tunisian street vendor, Mohamed Bouazizi, was confronted by local authorities for operating a produce cart without a permit. Conflicting witness testimonies claim he was disrespected by the police, requested bribery to ignore his lack of permit, slapped and spat on, had his produce thrown on the ground, and/or weighing scales confiscated. Regardless of what actually happened, Bouazizi went to the local official's office to complain. He was quoted as saying, "How do you expect me to make a living?" Despite this, Bouazizi was ignored. He threatened to set himself on fire if his situation continued to be suppressed through inaction. Enraged by the lack of concern for his personal and professional well-being, Bouazizi left and returned with a can of gasoline; he then lit himself on fire. He died of complications within a week.[117]

Within hours of the self-immolation, protests began in Bouazizi's hometown of Sidi Bouzid. By the time of his death, these protests had grown in size and scope. This sparked a series of protests,

---

[117] Thessa Lageman, "Remembering Mohamed Bouazizi: The Man Who Sparked the Arab Spring."

demonstrations, riots, and uprisings across North Africa and the Middle East known as the Arab Spring. Many young people of the regions were frustrated with the lack of economic opportunities or civil liberties. They took out their frustrations on the current governments who were viewed as the oppressors.

During this time, some government and media outlets attempted to censor the developing story. Some governments like Syria used violent crackdowns as a way to repress the uprising. Many governments pulled a play from their propaganda playbook in order to control the narrative surrounding the protest. Many media outlets were critical of the developing revolution while some showed sympathy for the movement's supporters. Some countries such as Tunisia and Egypt had government-controlled media where they were able to provide misinformation in order to sway public opinion. Other mainstream media organizations did not give it much thought or airtime.[118]

This lack of support to share the revolutionary story from outsiders led protestors to find their own way to circumvent censorship. Many protestors began using social media platforms such as Facebook, Twitter, and YouTube to share firsthand accounts of their side of the story. With these tools, protestors were better able to organize, mobilize, and share their opinions to help onlookers develop a balanced opinion over the unfolding events. Social media allowed the population a way to bypass government censorship.[119]

This didn't stop governments from trying to further suppress the uprising's communication with each other and the outside world. The Egyptian government at one point shut down their internet and mobile phone networks. Despite the blackout, Egyptian citizens were able to leverage technology like proxy servers to continue accessing these social media sites.[120]

---

[118] Haythem Guesmi, "The Social Media Myth About the Arab Spring."
[119] Korhan Kocak and Özgür Kıbrıs, "Social Media and Press Freedom."
[120] Kristen McTighe, "A Blogger at Arab Spring's Genesis."

Through the use of social media, locals were able to resist the censorship thrust upon them. Sharing the violence and repression they were under helped shape international opinion. By seeing what these people were dealing with, society was better able to be more informed and come together to put overwhelming pressure on the repressive governments. Calls for more freedom and democracy won out as a direct result of unfettered social media usage.

Edward Snowden

In 2013, Edward Snowden had in his possession state secrets showing serious crimes committed by US government officials. Snowden believed the actions of the government violated individual privacy rights. Snowden has since shared that "one of the key things that actually motivated me was the growing realization that we in the United States government were increasingly making decisions that departed from the rule of law."[121] While Snowden knowingly went against the NSA mission to protect the sensitive information of the National Security Agency, he felt morally and ethically compelled to share this realization with the public.

While Snowden revealed classified information, he more importantly illuminated how the information was obtained. Operation Stellar Wind, the warrantless surveillance program started under President George W. Bush made it possible for the government to collect the data of any US citizen without due process; the government could do this under the pretext of possible terrorism. This upended the

---

[121] Edward Snowden, *Terminal F/Chasing Edward Snowden (2015)*, 9:15–9:27.

"presumption of innocence" principle, which has roots as far back as Roman, Taldmudic, and Islamic law.[122]

The government did this by tapping into the internet systems of US companies. By doing so, they were able to collect an enormous amount of data including financial transactions on US citizens. By also cozying up to technology giants such as Facebook and Google, they were able to collect real-time messages, email, and other information necessary for the capture of their assumed enemies. Because of this, the government had the ability to create a profile of anyone suspected of wrongdoings. They knew what they were saying, who they knew, where they've been, where they are, what they've been buying and selling, even if they were in fact a law-abiding citizen.

The US government charged Snowden with espionage, theft, and conversion of government property. Obviously, the NSA wanted their secrets kept secret in order to maintain the nation's security. So it was imperative for them to keep Snowden from releasing the files. This act of whistleblowing, the revealing of information illegal or immoral action of a public or private organization, kicked off a manhunt for Edward Snowden who was now on the run. He first escaped to Hong Kong. After the media got wind of his whereabouts, he wanted to leave but was worried about being detained at border patrol. With the help of WikiLeaks, a non-governmental organization that publishes anonymous news leaks, Snowden was able to escape Hong Kong officials despite their cooperation with the US State Department who was now trying to capture him. After making it somewhat safely to Moscow, Russia, the US revoked Snowden's passport, which forced him to be stuck in the Russian airport.[123]

At this point, Snowden with the continued support of Wikileaks unsuccessfully attempted to find asylum with over twenty other nations. It wasn't until Bolivian President Evo Morales took a trip to Russia that the tides turned. The US, under the assumption Morales was

---

[122] Ed Pilkington, "'Panic Made Us Vulnerable'."
[123] Juan Lindau, *Surveillance and the Vanishing Individual*, 93–109.

attempting to provide asylum, forced his return flight to land in order to inspect his plane. This was a crucial misstep in terms of optics for the United States. The forced landing of a neutral governmental plane led to Snowden being seen globally as the victim and the US being the aggressors. Russia has since offered Snowden asylum where he currently resides.

Edward's Snowden's actions shed light onto the level of censorship a nation will go to in order to maintain control. Regardless if you think he was right or wrong in leaking the information to the public, the actions of the United States government showed how far the powerful will go to silence those below them. Right or wrong, Snowden, with the help of filmmaker Laura Poitras, and journalists Barton Gellman and Glenn Greenwald, were able to share his revelations with the public.[124] The scepter of censorship had been lost while simultaneously the public was able to be more informed on the inner workings of government surveillance and its impacts on personal privacy.

---

[124] Dave Davies, "Journalist Who Helped Break Snowden's Story."

Censorship Resistance

"The first condition of progress is the removal of censorships."[125]
~ George Bernard Shaw

The development of social consciousness can only be furthered when the shackles of intellectual restrictions are removed. While there may be valid arguments for considering not sharing specific information with others, having a small group arbitrarily make those decisions for everyone generally leads to poor outcomes. When one takes away opportunities from individuals to make mistakes, those individuals also lose out on the opportunity to learn from said mistakes. These missed opportunities, extrapolated over decades, leads to intellectual, spiritual, and societal stagnation.

Despite that, some still believe they have the moral authority to tell others what information they can consume. That's bullshit; censorship isn't paternalist protection. Censorship is control. It's all well and good when the political party you support is controlling the access to information, but what most people don't realize is that they're giving those weapons to the next administration — which may not be led by their own side. This regulatory creep leads to an increasingly less free society. While the ideal solution to this might be extremely limited censorship, that world is not going to materialize any time soon. Regardless, we can work towards countering the current state of censorship through the use of censorship resistant tools we have available.

We can and should do this in order to get to a shared understanding of the truth. As George Orwell stated in his classic novel *1984*, "Freedom is the freedom to say that two plus two make four."[126] There's no amount of control that can make that mathematical fact

---

[125] George Bernard Shaw, "The Author's Apology" in *Mrs. Warren's Profession*, 40.
[126] George Orwell, *1984*, ch. 7.

untrue. As Julian Assange said, "No amount of coercive force will ever solve a math problem."[127] We now have protocols in place to resist censorship and support truth. Bitcoin represents truth. It simply produces the truth of transactions every ten minutes. Through its proof-of-work consensus algorithm, it resists attacks of the powerful or politically connected to change or conceal the truth for their benefit. With censorship resistance applied in this way, we all can learn, we all can grow, and we all can develop together and live as a free community of humanity.

---

[127] Julian Assange, *Cypherpunks*, 5.

Open Source Collaboration

"Many hands make light work."[128]
~ John Heywood

If you had an idea and wanted to turn it into reality, you might harken back to the old adage, "If you want something done right, you have to do it yourself." Seems reasonable. Your vision is clear and, if done properly, your own ideas and hard work will allow you to reap the rewards. There's nothing wrong with that. But as the above Heywood quote alludes to, you'd be missing out on a number of potential advantages.

As you'll read in this chapter, history has expressed that there are many benefits to opening up the collaborative process to the development of ideas and products. One benefit of open source software is its transparency. The source code can be examined, updated, and shared. Open source projects are customizable, which ultimately benefit the customers and their unique needs and wants. There is often a groundswell of community support as participants feel a sense of ownership. There's also the benefit of cost savings since the ideas are freely distributed. All of this leads to the real key of innovation. While innovation is certainly possible in closed, proprietary systems, by allowing for open source access projects benefit from society's immense untapped brain power. Now anyone and everyone with an innovative itch to scratch has a chance to help. And that help benefits everyone in the network.

You don't have to take my word for it. The following examples in history show that open source collaboration is superior to closed source, proprietary solutions. Moreover, they are more ethical. Open source software offers freedom equally to users and developers. It removes the barriers of rent-seeking often found in proprietary systems.

---

[128] John Heywood, *The Proverbs*, 409.

Future generations will not be hamstrung by previous generations' technological restrictions. They will be better able to add their own building blocks to society unhindered by past shortsightedness.

Liechtenstein

There are many ways to measure successful collaboration in regards to governments and countries. Of those, maintaining a preeminent GDP (Gross Domestic Product) per capita, hosting a high quality standard of living, maintaining local property rights, paying low income taxes, having low crime rates, next to no unemployment, and being essentially debt free would rightfully place Liechtenstein in the elite category of successful countries. But what does this have to do with open source collaboration? If you view the sharing of ideas in regards to governance on a spectrum, closed source governance aligns with autocratic systems and open source collaboration aligns more with democracy. Confoundingly, Liechtenstein's governmental structure contains both a monarchy and a direct democracy. Since the signing of their constitution in 1921, Liechtenstein has maintained the principle that the authority of the state is shared by both the prince as well as the people.[129]

---

[129] Michael Wohlgemuth, "Liechtenstein: A Tale of Unusual Sovereignty."

Putting aside the royalty for the moment, Liechtenstein's direct democracy works through bottom-up, grassroots community support. Liechtensteiners have the right to suggest amendments to their constitution, petition to change laws, write referendums against financial decisions made by the parliament, and even choose to dissolve parliament. In extreme cases, the people have the ability to vote the prince out of office and even dissolve the monarchy. Even more, parliament gave itself the power to submit decisions to the vote of its people. For example, Prince Hans-Adam II sent a constitutional revision to the people for a vote in 2003, which they approved.[130]

Granted, they still have a monarchy at the top of their government, which doesn't make sense on the face of it. The prince reserves the right to dismiss government officials and veto legal or financial decisions. All laws and treaties must have his consent. Despite all his power, the Liechtensteiners view the monarchy positively and as necessary to the stability and success of their country.[131]

This form of collaboration — albeit semi-open — is a feature, not a bug. Unlike many Western democracies, this open source collaboration automatically creates clear transparency between the government and their constituents. This transparency creates trust and community support. This style of open collaboration also allows for innovation and customizability. In order to increase youth engagement in politics, Liechtenstein established its Youth Parliament in 2003, which gave up to twenty-five youth members between the ages of fourteen and twenty-five the ability to present proposals to parliament. Liechtenstein's direct democracy allows for creative solutions to shape public policy.

For these reasons and more, Liechtenstein is a desirable place to live. In addition to its high standard of living, relative safety and security, economic opportunities, and low taxation, its beautiful

---

[130] CNN, "Prince Wins Liechtenstein Powers."
[131] Wouter Veenendaal, "The Curious Case of Liechtenstein: A Country Caught Between a Prince and Democracy." LSE Blog.

countryside and natural landscapes are nestled in the Alps mountain range. But what sets Liechtenstein apart is the citizens' ability to work together. Its open source nature allowed the best parts of humanity to express themselves together, collaboratively.

Richard M. Stallman & GNU

In the 1970s, the Massachusetts Institute of Technology had a problem: One of their few printers kept jamming. Unlike the printer of today where one could choose which job to print, a jam back then would cause every other print job in the queue to become backed up. The good people at MIT came up with a plan to implement a code shared with everyone for when the printer jammed. The message "The printer is jammed, please fix it" would be displayed. Then, anyone could fix it without wasting an extra trip up and down the hall.

Years later when MIT upgraded to a laser printer, one of the staff programmers, Richard M. Stallman, requested the source code to the jammed printer message. Surprisingly, his request was declined under the reasoning it was proprietary code. Stallman then requested a similar code from a neighboring university. They declined as well. In their defense, many MIT researchers had signed non-disclosure agreements (NDAs) and went on to form businesses that ran on code created during their time at MIT. Nonetheless, the lack of desire to share and help a fellow academic didn't sit well with Stallman.[132]

---

[132] Sam Williams, *Free as in Freedom*, ch. 1.

This episode in history motivated Stallman to create an operating system that would not only be transparent and customizable, but would be free and open source. To clarify, free software is a step beyond open source. Wikipedia describes Free and Open Source Software (FOSS) as software "where anyone is freely licensed to use, copy, study, and change the software in any way, and the source code is openly shared so that people are encouraged to voluntarily improve the design of the software."[133]

In 1983, Stallman released his vision for free software in the form of the GNU project, which was a free version of the Unix-based system. GNU in fact stands for "GNU's Not UNIX." Stallman shared his rationale in his 1985 *The GNU Manifesto*, "I consider that the golden rule requires that if I like a program I must share it with other people who like it. I cannot in good conscience sign a nondisclosure agreement or a software license Agreement. So that I can continue to use computers without violating my principles, I have decided to put together a sufficient body of free software so that I will be able to get along without any software that is not free."[134]

In addition to the GNU project, Stallman established the idea of *copyleft*, which, as Wikipedia states, "is the legal technique of granting certain freedoms over copies of copyrighted works with the requirement that the same rights be preserved in derivative works."[135] This contrasts its long-standing counterpart of copyright, which gives legal protection to various forms of intellectual property. Copyleft allowed for various levels of freedom to software developers. Freedom 0 is the freedom to use the work; Freedom 1 is the freedom to study the work; Freedom 2 is the freedom to copy and share the work with others; Freedom 3 is the freedom to modify the work, and the freedom to distribute modified and therefore derivative works.[136]

---

[133] Wikipedia, "Free and Open-source Software."
[134] Stallman, "Free Unix!"
[135] Wikipedia, "Copyleft."
[136] Free Software Foundation, "What Is Free Software?"

Thanks to the development of the GNU project, coders were liberated to effectively collaborate free from legal patent restrictions. Some of the projects that developed from this are as follows: GNU Compiler Collection (GCC), GNU Debugger (GDB), GNU Emacs, GNU Bison, GNU Make, and Apache HTTP Server. All of these tools provided a free way for developers to innovate free from the tediousness of coding. In addition, GNU/Linux was created, which is a free and open source operating system that connects the Linux kernel (a kernel is the main component of most computer operating systems) and the GNU utilities.

While these acronyms might seem meaningless to the nontechnical reader, these innovations have had a significant impact on the technology industry. Thanks to the pioneering spirit of Stallman, freedom from legal shackles in the digital realm became not only a possibility but also a goal. As Stallman eloquently states, "Free software is the first battle in the liberation of cyberspace."[137]

---

[137] Stallman, "Free Software, Free Society," (0:10–0:18).

Linus Torvalds & Linux

Thanks to copyright-based lawsuits by AT&T (against Berkeley Software Distribution) and Leica Development (against GNU Hurd), computer science student Linus Torvalds' kernel of an idea was planted. While studying at the University of Helsinki, he grew frustrated with the popular but proprietary operating systems (OS) of the time. Whether these lawsuits represented greed or close-mindedness, one thing is for sure: They had an inhibiting effect on innovation.

As a hobby, Linus Torvalds started creating his own OS. By 1991, Torvalds had compiled roughly ten thousand lines of source code which constituted the Linux kernel, the core of his free and open source OS. Channeling the phrase "if you love something, set it free," Torvalds released the source code into the wild by inviting other developers to inspect, modify, and redistribute.[138]

Within a year, the Linux kernel was paired with the aforementioned GNU project. As Torvaldis explained in the Linux release 0.01, "Sadly,

---

[138] Matthew Newton, "Is Linux Right For You?"

a kernel by itself gets you nowhere. To get a working system you need a shell, compilers, a library etc. These are separate parts and may be under a stricter (or even looser) copyright. Most of the tools used with linux are GNU software and are under the GNU copyleft."[139] In 1992, Torvalds moved to have Linux under the GNU general public license. Torvalds claimed this "was definitely the best thing I ever did."[140] Doing so allowed developers to create a complete OS free of cost to the world.

By 1994, Linux 1.0.0 was released, which was new and improved thanks to contributions by close to twelve thousand programmers. What started as ten thousand lines of code had blossomed to over 175,000 lines of code, all of which were still completely free to use. This marriage of two free and open software projects led to an explosion of distributions.[141] Today, Linux (more specifically Linux/GNU) can be found in server hosting, web development, scientific computing, cloud computing, gaming, and the Internet of Things (IoT). One of the most popular mobile operating systems, Android, is based on a modified version of the Linux kernel.

Despite it being mainly used by the technical community due to its complexity, Linux is widely considered to be the best OS around. Not only is it free and open source, its customizability allows for developers to tailor it for specific user needs. Linux is a remarkably stable OS. It hardly crashes or has viruses, which are the norm for other not-to-be-named operating systems. On top of all that, Linux is extremely secure due to the community of developers being able to review the code. Its compatibility allows anyone and everyone the ability to run a wide range of applications. Torvalds summed up the idea of FOSS rather well when he said "software is like sex: it's better when it's free."[142]

---

[139] Linus Torvalds, "Notes for Linux Release 0.01."
[140] Hiroo Yamargata, "The Pragmatist of Free Software: Linus Torvalds Interview."
[141] Jae Yun Moon and Lee Sproull, "Essence of Distributed Work."
[142] Linus Torvalds, "Software is Like Sex: It's Better When it's Free."

Sal Khan & Khan Academy

In 2004, Sal's younger cousin was having issues learning sixth-grade math, so he offered to tutor her long-distance using tools ranging from the old-fashioned phone call to *Yahoo!* Doodle Images and Instant Messenger. Soon enough, another of Sal's cousins asked for help, then another. Eventually, the number of cousins in Sal's after-work "classroom" reached double digits. A friend of Sal's, realizing the time constraints of such a benevolent endeavor, suggested Sal record himself teaching various lessons and post them on YouTube.[143] Initially, Sal thought this was a horrible idea. In his own words, Sal originally thought "YouTube is for cats playing piano. It's not for serious mathematics."[144] After getting over the idea that it wasn't his idea, Sal gave it a shot.

Throughout the following few years, many non-family members began following, watching, and commenting on Sal's videos. Many comments were gracious in nature, thanking Sal for helping them better

---

[143] Salman Khan, *The One World Schoolhouse*, 4–6.
[144] Sal Khan, "Education Reimagined," 2.

themselves free of charge. Having graduated from Massachusetts Institute of Technology (MIT) and Harvard Business School, Sal had the intellect and tools needed to take this idea to the next level. Realizing not only the benefit to offering free educational content but also the scalability thanks to the various digital tools available gave Sal the motivation he needed. It is from this that Khan Academy was born.

Launched in 2008, Khan Academy began as a not-for-profit organization (NFPO). Sal had quit his then job as an investment firm analyst in order to achieve his goal. At the time, Sal was living off savings until 2010 when large philanthropic support began flooding in. Organizations such as the Gates Foundation, Google, and the Broad Foundation reached out in support. From there, Khan Academy matured from educational videos to a free and open interactive platform providing feedback, tools for teachers, and unlimited practice for people to achieve mastery across a multitude of topics. The topics currently covered in Khan Academy, all of which are free to anyone with Internet access, range from K-12 basic math, higher level collegiate mathematics, biology, chemistry, physics, computer programming, reading and language arts, economics, history, and other life skills.[145]

Khan Academy's source code for their online learning platform uses MIT's open source license, which allows educators and developers the ability to access, modify, and share materials and code freely with anyone.[146] This liberates motivated individuals to innovate and collaborate in the name of education. Furthermore, it offers a refreshing view of the nature of education. As the quote apocryphally attributed to Mark Twain goes, "I never let school get in the way of my education."[147] In the same vein, Khan Academy allows individuals the ability to learn and grow in whatever area of study interests them. No

---

[145] Colleen Walsh, "Education Without Limits."

[146] Khan Academy, "Creative Commons and Open Source."

[147] Garson O'Toole, "Never Let Schooling Interfere With Your Education."

longer do we need to focus solely on test scores pertinent only to administrators and bureaucrats in order to grow. Rather, we can attain mastery for which we are intimately passionate.

Jimmy Wales & Wikipedia

Inspired by the ideas of Adam Smith (who contributed to the concept of spontaneous order, phenomenon that are the result of human action but not of human design) and FA Hayek (who argued language, money, the common law, the moral code, and trade result from spontaneous order), Jimmy Wales believed in the value of local knowledge outweighing that of central authority. In 2000, Jimmy Wales and Larry Sanger created a free online encyclopedia called Nupedia. Contributors were considered experts in their field. This endeavor was meant to rival the burgeoning Encyclopedia Britannica, whose website was generating a good amount of relative traffic. Nupedia's goal to oust Encyclopedia Britannica through a free, peer-reviewed model was admirable. Unfortunately, due to multiple factors such as the dot-com crash, poor funding, and an arduous peer-review process, Nupedia shut down in 2003. Despite millions of dollars in funding, it had only published a couple dozen articles throughout its entire existence.[148]

---

[148] Andrew Lih, *The Wikipedia Revolution*, 13–37.

Launched in 2001, Wales and Sanger also created Wikipedia but did so with the intent to make it a discussion forum for what information should be submitted to Nupedia. The word wiki is Hawaiian for "quick." The concept of a wiki dates back to 1994 when Ward Cunningham created the first online wiki, which is a website whose content is open sourced. Since Wikipedia was indeed a wiki, anyone was able to create, edit, or discuss potential content. By the end of Nupedia, Wikipedia had created over 20,000 articles in its first year alone. While Jimmy Wales believed the open model of Wikipedia was a potentially superior model, Larry Sanger disagreed and thus the two went their separate ways.[149]

Wikipedia has no advertisements, which, in a sense, makes it less prone to bias or audience capture compared to other sources of information. For example, if a search engine was funded by a pharmaceutical company, there would be an incentive for the search engine to promote said pharmaceutical company as a solution to any relevant searches. On the other hand, Wikipedia chose the non-profit route, thus receiving funding through its Wikimedia Foundation as well as donations.

While Wikipedia is indeed a free, collaborative platform, it is not without tradeoffs. Some choose not to access their wide range of topics due to concerns of accuracy. Because of its wiki nature, anyone can edit articles, which has the potential to provide misinformation. While that is a common feeling among Wikipedia's detractors, evidence supports the opposite is true. Multiple scientific articles across many sources have suggested that Wikipedia is in fact as or more accurate than other encyclopedias such as Britannica.[150] In addition, Wikipedia articles are chocked full of citations and references. There's even a

[149] Lily Rothman, "Wikipedia at 15: How the Concept of a Wiki Was Invented."
[150] Imogen Casebourne et al. "Assessing the Accuracy and Quality of Wikipedia Entries"; Jim Giles, "Internet Encyclopaedias."

Wikipedia page titled "Reliability of Wikipedia" that discusses its validity.[151]

There are currently more than 6.6 million articles in over 250 languages on Wikipedia making it the world's largest encyclopedia.[152] Wikipedia echoes how reality is formed, similar to how language is emergent. There is not a small, select few privileged individuals dictating from on high what the definition of words or concepts are. Language and thus reality are rather emergent through countless iterations, uses, and discussions. It's spontaneous and sometimes sloppy, but the most recent iteration is usually more grounded than a potentially damaging decree from an ivory tower. The best perceptions and descriptions are generally accepted in the collective consciousness. Cream rises to the top, which takes time.

[151] Wikipedia, "Reliability of Wikipedia."
[152] Manish Singh, "Wikipedia."

Open Source Collaboration

"Given enough eyeballs, all bugs are shallow."[153]
~ Eric S. Raymond

Evolution will happen with or without us. We have the ability to increase not only its efficiency but also its equity. By promoting the use of open source solutions, we are promoting transparency, and accountability. We are promoting an inclusive, collaborative, and community-focused mindset. We are promoting cost-effective solutions to increase innovation.

Would you rather live in a world where everything from products to policy are obfuscated and behind the curtain? Granted, there are many things that don't necessarily need to be laid out for all to see. But what about money (namely the supply thereof), the one asset that touches everything in society? Shouldn't there be open source systems in place allowing for the best ideas to rise to the top?

This isn't *The Wizard of Oz* where a select few have proprietary control over the economic controls shouting "pay no attention to that man behind the curtain!" We all should at least have the ability to inspect and modify. If there's a better form of money available, let the people choose. In that situation, which obviously would be an ongoing, iterative process, society would be free to customize and innovate. Network effects would take over, innovation would occur, and cream would eventually rise to the top.

---

[153] Eric Raymond, *The Cathedral & The Bazaar*, 19.

Immutability

"What is once well done is done forever."[154]
~ Henry David Thoreau

Many of us have something to say, a song to sing, an image to display, or an idea to share. Some of these are worthy enough to share with the world. An even smaller amount can and should live on for eternity. It is to these ends that history has worked towards creating the permanence of culture.

In addition to this need to infinitely save our identity, there's also the need to keep the truth alive for those that might benefit from its suppression. Similar to the property of censorship resistance discussed in chapter 5, history has shown the desire to resist the ability of powerful people to eradicate instances of information to their own advantage.

Even more so, there are certain constants in the universe that have shown themselves as immutable. Despite attempts to disprove or replace them, their permanence remains. The following times in history point towards ways to create immortality with respect to the laws governing nature.

---

[154] Henry David Thoreau, "Civil Disobedience," 24.

Petroglyphs

Dating back to the Neanderthals roughly 65,000 years ago we have been finding ways to preserve our expressions of thought. With the inception of petroglyphs, carved drawings inside caves, early mankind had the ability to communicate crucial concepts. Similar to the emojis of today, petroglyphs were graphical representations of thoughts and values. They were most likely the first instantiation of humans to transmit and save a message across time.

Petroglyphs were made with a variety of tools. From materials such as sand and small rocks to stone chisels and metals later on.[155] Cave walls were also decorated by various pigments such as plant matter, charcoal, and minerals. Even fire was used to design drawings by directing the heat towards the desired area.[156] All of these techniques were attempts to find the most efficient way to create a durable account of history.[157]

---

[155] Robert Bednarik, "The Technology of Petroglyphs."
[156] Ben Guarino, "The Oldest Story Ever Told."
[157] Douglas Bird and Rebecca Bird. "Signalling Theory and Durable Symbolic Expression," 356.

Although we can only speculate as to the reasons for the drawings, we can still appreciate the drawings thanks to the durability of materials used. Often animals were featured. Depending on the time in history as well as the cave's location, animals such as mammoths, bison, horses, deer, lions, and bears were displayed. Some believe these were created for survival purposes. Depictions of nature were common in caves. Landforms, weather patterns, and even stars might have helped them develop their understanding of the world in which they lived.[158] Activities including hunting, dancing, and spiritual rituals were inscribed possibly in order to preserve their memories. There is also much evidence of geometric and abstract shapes being displayed throughout the world. While their purpose may be interpreted in many ways, there's no denying petroglyphs have stood the test of time.

These timeless transcriptions have withstood thousands of years. Petroglyphs' property of immutability have allowed them to sustain the record of past civilizations, culture, and values. Having a snapshot into the past allows us to connect with previous generations. We are better able to learn from history when said history is maintained in the form the originator intended. In that respect, beliefs and cultures are respected, free from potential revisionism.

Imagine losing your identity thus your place in history due to an alterable archive. Extrapolate the potential negative externalities over specific cultures or entire generations.[159] Without immutability, your race or your people's history could be erased. It's no surprise the humans responsible for petroglyphs used tools on their cavernous canvases to combat the possibility of misrepresentation or, even worse, obsolescence. As time marches on, there will remain a need for improving ways to provide immutability for humanity.

---

[158] Jo Marchant, "A Journey to the Oldest Cave Paintings in the World."
[159] Leslie Zubieta, "The Role of Rock Art as Mnemonic Device."

Ten Commandments

Known as one of the most well-established set of immutable rules, the Ten Commandments have endured many attacks across multiple centuries. The Ten Commandments, which are foundational in Jewish, Christian, and Islamic traditions, are as follows…

1. You shall have no other gods before Me.
2. You shall make no idols.
3. You shall not take the name of the Lord your God in vain.
4. Keep the Sabbath day holy.
5. Honor your father and your mother.
6. You shall not murder.
7. You shall not commit adultery.
8. You shall not steal.
9. You shall not bear false witness against your neighbor.
10. You shall not covet.

This list of virtuous behaviors is believed to have been handed down by God to Moses on Mount Sinai approximately 3,500 years ago.[160] These commandments were seen as necessary for societies to behave morally and orderly. While open to interpretation, these principles have shown their immutability.

According to the Bible, the Ten Commandments had been inscribed by God on two stone tablets. They didn't last long, though. Moses received these tablets while leading the Israelites out of Egypt. Unfortunately, the Israelites impatiently chose to worship a golden calf. This enraged Moses who ended up throwing the tablets on the ground, resulting in their destruction. As stated in Exodus 32:19-20 (NIV), "When Moses approached the camp and saw the calf and the dancing, his anger burned and he threw the tablets out of his hands, breaking them to pieces at the foot of the mountain. And he took the calf the people had made and burned it in the fire; then he ground it to powder, scattered it on the water and made the Israelites drink it." Afterwards, Moses went back up the mountain to get another set of tablets from God. This copy is what was preserved in the Ark of the Covenant.

Despite the immutability of the Ten Commandments' underlying concepts, the medium for many of the original copies were less durable. The popular material for inscribing at the time was parchment paper, the untanned skins of animals. As with any organic matter, it decays over time. That provided a challenge for historians attempting to maintain one of the most sacred documents in history. Some historians unsuccessfully tried to keep pieces together using everyday adhesive tape. Unbeknown to them at the time, the tape's residue led to the parchment disintegrating further.

While many copies suffered from Mother Nature's unrelenting ways, the moral code embedded in the Ten Commandments was able to endure eternity. Like nodes in a network, these ideas were passed on by people from generation to generation. This form of immutability, the persistence of ideas, are oftentimes better able to withstand the test of time than physical items. Good ideas are hard to destroy…

---

[160] Brian Duignan, "Ten Commandments."

Newton's Laws of Motion

At nine years old, Sir Isaac Newton created his first sundial. By his mid-twenties, he invented calculus. In his thirties, he discovered light was a composite of all colors. Looking back at his intellectual arc, it's no surprise Sir Isaac Newton would someday be the one to discover the laws of physics.[161]

Published in 1687, Newton's *Philosophiæ Naturalis Principia Mathematica* (also known as *Principia)* detailed his laws of motion and universal gravitation. Newton's first law states "A body remains at rest, or in motion at a constant speed in a straight line, unless acted upon by a force." Imagine if you were playing catch in space. With the force of gravity very miniscule, the ball you throw would go in the same direction forever provided it doesn't bump into anything or another larger or close object's gravity took control. Newton's second law states "When a body is acted upon by a force, the time rate of change of its momentum equals the force." So there's an actual equation now to show the harder you hit a ball, the further it will go. Finally,

---

[161] James Langham, "Sir Isaac Newton," 357–58.

Newton's third law states "If two bodies exert forces on each other, these forces have the same magnitude but opposite directions." This means the force of the bat on the ball is equal to the force of the ball on the bat.

As with any scientific theory, the solidity of Newton's laws have been subject to criticism. There have been many attempts to revise, refine, and refute these laws of motion. In the early twentieth century, Albert Einstein proposed his Theory of General Relativity. Without geeking out too much, Einstein added the idea of spacetime curvature, which led to the famous $E=mc^2$. While this is a more accurate statement of Newton's laws — especially for massive objects — the basis for them remained intact. Also in the early twentieth century, Niels Bohr helped develop the branch of physics known as quantum mechanics. This branch of physics focused on atoms and subatomic particles. Some quantum concepts even challenged Newton's classical notion of causality.[162] Even more recently are the concepts of dark matter and dark energy, which focus on observations of the universe. These hypothetical forms of matter once again challenged Newton's laws by suggesting invisible matter and energy influence gravity's effect on the universe. While these alternative takes on physics challenged Newton's classical mechanics, none of them stopped the laws of motion from occurring. If anything, physics has been strengthened thanks to these examples of further scientific discovery.[163]

Notice how none of Newton's laws were decreed and then expected to be free from criticism. It was centuries of rigorous scientific experimentation that led humanity to concluding that these laws were immutable. The fundamental concepts of classical mechanics that were developed in the seventeenth century are still used today. It is for these reasons we can consider Newton's laws of motion immutable. As we continue through history, we should continue to incorporate immutable

---

[162] Sabine Hossenfelder, "Head Trip."
[163] Adrian Cho, "Can Dark Matter Vanquish a Rival Theory?"

truths while casting away wasteful endeavors. Newton famously said "Plato is my friend, Aristotle is my friend, but my greatest friend is truth."[164] We should all aspire to adopt systems that crystallize truth throughout time.

---

[164] Isaac Newton, "Questiones Quædam Philosophiæ."

Watergate Scandal

In 1972, US President Richard Millhouse Nixon ran for reelection against his opponent, Democrat George McGovern. Concerned with the waning chances of securing a second term, Nixon's staff felt compelled to act. The Committee for the Re-Election of the President (CRP, mockingly named CREEP) broke into the Democratic National Committee (DNC) headquarters located in The Watergate Hotel in Washington, DC. The presidential aides stole top secret documents as well as wiretapped the DNC office. Hotel security noticed many of the door locks were taped over, which prompted them to contact the authorities. The criminals were promptly detained.

Before the end of the calendar year, journalists Carl Bernstein and Bob Woodward of the *Washington Post* published allegations by the (Federal Bureau of Investigation) FBI that Nixon's aides were responsible for the crimes. Although implicated, Richard Nixon was never convicted for crimes during Watergate. He was associated with the following crimes: In addition to the burglary (theft and wiretapping), Nixon and his aides engaged in conspiracy and obstruction of justice; they attempted to pay hush money to the burglars, gave misinformation during the investigation, and ordered the destruction of evidence. Nixon was accused of abuse of power by using the FBI and Central Intelligence Agency (CIA) to harass political opponents. Nixon's previously mentioned CRP were also found guilty of campaign finance violations by accepting illegal contributions. If that wasn't enough, Nixon was charged with contempt of Congress by not complying with subpoenas nor offering requested documents during the investigation.[165]

When Nixon resigned from office in 1974, he became the first US president to do so. His aides were found guilty and imprisoned for their actions during the Watergate scandal. You might be wondering what this has to do with immutability. One aspect of immutability shown in this historic episode is that the legal systems were in fact mutable. Those expected to uphold the law were the ones who abused their responsibilities through illegal activities as well as obfuscatory tactics. Thanks to Watergate, the idea that our rule of law is immutable has been tainted. This, in addition to many other episodes in history, lead to the public's distrust of government. Those in power are not immune to human flaws, corruption, deceit, or abuse of power.

The Watergate scandal illuminated that no person, regardless of power or prestige was capable of suppressing the truth. Even the most powerful and seemingly immutable institutions and individuals can be subject to scrutiny, accountability, and change. It is for reasons like these that the perception of the immutability of government institutions is shattered. It is for reasons like these that we should aspire to promote the adoption of systems that remove human fallibility. It is for reasons like these that we should continue to build upon the strong foundations of immutable protocols.

---

[165] Carl Bernstein and Bob Woodward, *All the President's Men.*

Julian Assange

In 2010, US Army intelligence analyst, Private First Class Manning, was arrested in Iraq for being suspected of leaking thousands of classified state documents to WikiLeaks, a non-profit organization that publishes classified information and leaks from anonymous sources with the goal of promoting transparency and government accountability. Under the direction of Julian Assange, WikiLeaks released a series of leaked documents known as the "Iraq War Logs" and "Afghan War Diary," which contained classified information about the US military's actions in Iraq and Afghanistan.[166]

These leaked documents exposed potential war crimes committed by the US military such as incidents of civilian casualties, abuse, and extrajudicial killings. They illustrated human rights abuses, including torture and mistreatment of detainees, by US forces and their allies. The documents raised questions about the level of transparency and accountability within the US government, including concerns about the classification and handling of sensitive information.

---

[166] Amanda Holpuch, "Chelsea Manning."

Suffice to say, this did not please the US military complex. With the growing risk of extradition, Assange sought asylum in the Embassy of Ecuador in London in 2012 and remained there for seven years. By 2019, Assange was arrested by British authorities after Ecuador revoked his asylum. Assange was then sentenced to fifty weeks in prison for breaching bail conditions. Within the following months, the US Department of Justice charged Assange with multiple counts of violating the Espionage Act for his role in publishing classified information, including the leaks from Private Manning. Since 2019, Assange has been detained in London after being expelled from the Ecuadorian embassy. As of this writing, Julian is still fighting extradition to the United States.[167]

The story of Julian Assange and WikiLeaks represents immutability in many ways. The preservation of information is crucial in determining truth. Once information is leaked to the public and disseminated, the original content cannot be changed. Thanks to WikiLeaks, the suppression of truth by abusers of power is diminished, which also increases transparency, whether warranted or unwarranted. WikiLeaks follows a strict policy of not editing or altering the leaked information in any way, which ensures that the leaked information remains immutable and authentic. Despite the numerous legal battles Assange and WikiLeaks have faced, their information remains unchanged.[168]

Assange once said, "Nearly every war that has started in the past fifty years has been a result of media lies."[169] Imagine if we had the ability as a society to immutably record accurate transactions for eternity. Having a system with the ability to promote truth and disallow lies would eradicate the potential for those in power to increase their power via the means of warfare.

---

[167] Peter Chawaga, "Free Assange."
[168] Jonathan Zittrain, "Technology Lessons from the Wikileaks Saga."
[169] Alvin Foo, "Nearly Every War."

Immutability

"Immutable money permanently unmutes the voice of the people." [170]
~ Robert Breedlove

Notice how the early humans that created petroglyphs didn't choose to make smiley poop emojis. It is assumed they were intent on memorializing what they found valuable. They did so with the best tools and mediums available. As time went on and humans developed their cognitive and spiritual capacity, we found greater and more in-depth concepts to share. Simultaneously, we evolved our ability to conserve these concepts. This is the arc of history.

Promoting protocols that value immutability is the necessary next step in our history. Wouldn't finding a way to guarantee your existence lead to an increase in feelings of trust and security? Immutability leads to value preservation as we are better able to save what we want for as long as necessary. We're better able as a society to come to a shared consensus with all data available to everyone, which leads to further transparency and accountability.

Truth should be immutable. If we truly want a fair and just society, we should allow light to shine on the public entities that govern us. Without it, we give up any semblance of checks and balances; there's no quality assurance when a specific group can say what is true or untrue, relevant or irrelevant, information or misinformation. It's necessary to point out that this idea speaks to all political parties. By giving "your side" the ability to subdue whatever they want, you're tacitly giving the same power to the "other side" when they return to power. Immutability is one of the properties required to combat this misuse of narrative control.

---

[170] Robert Breedlove, "Immutable Money."

Scarcity

"The first lesson of economics is scarcity:
there is never enough of anything to fully satisfy all those who want it.
The first lesson of politics is to disregard the first lesson of
economics."[171]
~ Thomas Sowell

It's a common assertion that scarcity is a reminder to appreciate what we have; we tend to cherish the things in our life that are rare more than the things that are plentiful. Scarcity refers to the insufficiency of amount or supply of a thing. Throughout history, humans have valued those things that display the property of scarcity, even if the thing wasn't indeed scarce. No? Ever heard of Beanie Babies? Or NFTs? Said differently, value is subjective, but by zooming out on history, we can see that those things that are actually scarce tend to be more highly valued.

The need to value scarcity has driven economists to create models and equations around scarcity. Supply and demand is a model in economics that helps market participants determine the price of a good partly based on its scarcity and partly on consumer desire to purchase said goods. Even the study of economics is a study of scarcity. English economist Lionel Robbins once wrote, "Economics is the science which studies human behaviour as a relationship between ends and scarce means which have alternative uses."[172]

Another economic consideration is the law of diminishing marginal utility, which states that any added utility gained from increased consumption decreases with each subsequent increase in the level of consumption: The usefulness of a thing goes down as market participants consume more of that thing. This results in the perceived

---

[171] Thomas Sowell, *Is Reality Optional?*, 131.
[172] Lionell Robbins, *An Essay on the Nature and Significance of Economic Science*, 15.

---

value and price decreasing as consumers are less willing to pay for the more easily consumed thing.

This chapter takes a slight departure from the theme of history echoing the properties that constitute Bitcoin. The following sections are less about specific episodes in history and more about concepts and items that have either exemplified or provided a non-example of the property of scarcity throughout history.

Time

Time is linear, meaning it continues from the past through the present and into the future in a straight line. No going back; no skipping forward. Without it, we would not be able to communicate in regards to events. We couldn't say "when did that happen?" With it, humans have been able to better understand the world throughout multiple scientific disciplines. Time helps us describe how energy is transferred and transformed. It helps us understand how the universe evolves and changes. Time provides direction. It cannot be replenished. It is the most scarce aspect of our life.

Over two thousand years ago, Greek philosopher Theophrastus stated "Time is the most valuable thing a man can spend."[173] He understood wasting time is the most costly thing one can do. Hundreds of years later, the Talmud (primary source of Jewish law) recognized the principle of opportunity cost. It advised that a person should consider the opportunity cost of waiting and make a decision based on their individual circumstances. Benjamin Franklin echoed this when he

---

[173] Philip Zimbardo and John Boyd, *The Time Paradox*, 27.

said "Time is money."[174] He was referring to opportunity cost, which is what is foregone when making a decision. This is a key component of the time value of money, which is a calculation that helps one determine if there is greater benefit to receiving a thing of value now rather than an identical amount later. Those individuals who can make sound decisions by deferring gratification in the present tend to receive a greater reward in the future.

People who hold this mindset have what is called low time preference. Individuals who express a low time preference are more likely to save for future generations, consider building reliable systems that stand the test of time, and resist the temptation to "get rich quick." These are the people that take time to follow the proverb "If you give a man a fish, you feed him for a day. If you teach a man to fish, you feed him for a lifetime." They are the teachers and learners of, not only the act of *fishing,* but the developers of *fishing technologies* that free up our time for other meaningful endeavors. Individuals with low time preference consistently craft default actions around them, which frees up their time to do the more meaningful things in life like play catch with their child.

This is contrasted with the concept of high time preference where individuals focus on feeding immediate needs and desires. These are the people that impulse buy, that emotionally and immediately react to intense stimuli, that ignore their future needs for the desires of the present. Consider Maslow's hierarchy of needs, which is a framework that describes the growth stages in humans. People with high time preference tend to get stuck in the lower levels of the pyramid (physiological and safety needs) and never evolve to the higher levels (self-actualization and transcendence). This is similar to the concept of poverty mindset where individuals get stuck in a cycle of fear, which prevents them from being able to exit the cycle of worry and negativity. Unfortunately, their personal growth is stunted because their time is used inefficiently because they focus on immediate existential threats.

---

[174] Benjamin Franklin, "Advice to a Young Tradesman."

Extrapolate this to entire communities over generations, and we have a severe impediment to the evolution of society.

Because time is scarce, we must work towards using the time we have efficiently. As we all know, we can't make more time for ourselves. This temporal limit can be considered a blessing if we view it as a motivating factor for us to take action. In order to do so, we should embrace systems that allow us the maximum amount of time possible to do what we love. That's hard to do, though, when the default actions we have in place increasingly require more of our time and attention. As we will discuss in the forthcoming sections, some developments in history (fiat) have robbed us of our time while others (bitcoin) offer hope towards a future filled with an abundance of time.

Podcaster and co-host of Mass Adoption Bitcoin Meetup, Conor Chepenik, summarizes this previous point particularly well, "There is no way to accurately account for all the wasted time fiat has brung about but it's clear if our money was not stolen from us via legal money counterfeiting the increased productivity would flow back to all of humanity and everyone would have more time to do what they wanted because their money was not losing purchasing power so rapidly. Exponential growth is hard to grasp and if we had a sound base layer it would mean humanity would have exponentially more time."[175]

---

[175] Conor Chepenik, personal correspondence with the author.

Gold

As far back as 2600 BC, the Ancient Egyptians understood the concept of scarcity and the need for an asset to store wealth. They began using gold as a standard value and stored it in their royal treasury.[176] Around 600 BC, the minting of gold coins began to spread throughout the Mediterranean region.[177] What the people of that era began to realize is that gold is not only scarce but durable and portable. Gold quickly began playing a significant role in the development of civilizations. This reality has lasted for millennia.

Gold is considered scarce because it is relatively rare compared to other elements on Earth. In order to extract gold from the Earth's crust, miners must make a significant investment in specialized and expensive machinery. Even with all global miners' infrastructure, its supply only increases (aka, inflates) a few percent per year. Said differently, gold boasts a high stock-to-flow ratio. This is a ratio used to measure the current supply of a commodity in circulation relative to

[176] Rosmarie Klemm and Dietrich Klemm, "Gold and Gold Mining in Ancient Egypt and Nubia," 21–27.

[177] Joseph Milne, "The Currency of Egypt Under the Ptolemies."

the amount that is produced annually. Gold's stock-to-flow ratio is high, meaning that it has a large existing stock relative to its annual production. Gold's historical predictability mixed with its scarcity is in part why governments chose to use it as a base money for their currencies.

At the beginning of the sixteenth century, Christopher Columbus made the following quote in a letter to his patrons, King Ferdinand and Queen Isabella of Spain: "Gold is a treasure, and he who possesses it does all he wishes to in this world, and succeeds in helping souls into paradise."[178] In his letter, Columbus wrote about the importance of finding gold and other valuable resources in the New World as a means to security and success. It seems as if he intuited how the scarcity of gold provided a physical instantiation of preserved time; the process of obtaining gold was a way for Columbus to store time and effort.

Despite all of gold's trimmings, there have been limiting factors to its continued use as the most scarce and valuable asset. One factor is its physical limitations. While gold is relatively good at storing value over time, it lacks in its ability to be transported over distance. Imagine how much it would cost to send $1,000,000 or more of gold across continents. Economist and Bitcoin educator Saifedean Ammous mentions a $3,000 price quote he received from a gold dealer for shipping a gold bar across the Atlantic (at current market prices, a standard gold bar fetches upward of $900,000, for little less than half a percent of shipping cost).[179] Also add the cost for security and all the trust issues involved in that process. How long would you assume this transaction would take? As discussed in chapter one, government capture is also a limit on gold's perceived value in that personal ownership is constantly at risk of confiscation by governments who don't highly value its constituents' property rights.

Warts and all, gold has historically been the, well... gold standard of scarce assets and thus a valuable asset. In order to obtain gold, one

---

[178] Christóbal Colon, "The Fourth Voyage of Columbus."
[179] Saifedean Ammous, *The Fiat Standard*, 81–82.

131

must prove some amount of work. Gold is not something that can easily be replicated or rehypothecated (besides "paper gold," IOUs for gold). It is a bearer asset that can only be obtained by mining it, providing some service, or by buying it with previously-earned capital (assuming you don't have the power to print your own). As Ron Paul once said, "Because gold is honest money, it is disliked by dishonest men."[180] That honesty comes in the form of our time and effort; gold's value comes from its scarcity, which comes from its proof of work.

---

[180] Ron Paul, *The Case for Gold*, 183.

Fiat

Fiat money is a currency that has value not because it is backed by something physical like gold or silver, but because a government declares it to be legal tender. It is for this that the meaning of the term "fiat" is "by decree." As far back as seventh-century China, fiat money has been used.

The United States holds the record for the largest and longest-running fiat monetary experiment. As a result of the economic conditions caused by World War II, the Bretton Woods system was created. This system pegged the value of most major currencies to the dollar with the dollar being convertible to gold. As the US government did what governments do (print dollars to pay for things in the short term, thereby inflating the supply), inflationary pressure began to mount.

In 1971, US President Richard Nixon declared that the dollar would no longer be convertible to gold. It was at this point Bretton Woods was over and the United States tried its hand at conducting our current fiat monetary experiment. After the US converted to this style of money, most major currencies have changed to a fully fiat currency.

Fiat's value comes partly from supply and demand in foreign exchange markets, partly from the threat of violence (governments can, have, and will impose punishment, fines, or imprisonment to a citizen for violating currency laws or regulations), and partly from public receivability (governments demand that you pay taxes in their currency).

Despite its lack of backing by a physical object like gold, fiat money is currently the dominant form of money. It has historically been transacted in the form of paper but has become overwhelmingly digital in recent decades.[181] As a result of the departure from being backed by gold, it is becoming increasingly easy for governments to manipulate its supply. As Federal Reserve Chair Jerome Powell has stated, "As a central bank, we have the ability to create money digitally."[182] This severely damages fiat's ability to be scarce. This seemingly infinite ability to inflate supply leads to currency debasement; fiat's lack of scarcity hinders its ability to economically store time and effort. This framing also can help us understand why we have seen massive inflation in countries around the world over the past fifty years.

Another factor limiting fiat's perception of scarcity and value stems from its current preferred use by governments as "political currency units." A phrase coined by Luke Broyles, political currency units refer to any governments' fiat that have discarded the scarcity money historically provided under the gold standard in favor of a new form of fiat money that is given perceived value from its use in currying political favors as well as synthetically created legitimacy.[183] What incentive, outside of avoiding fear of further restriction, does any individual have to assign value to such a tool (sans the wielder of the weapon)? Said differently, the tool of fiat is no longer used primarily for store of value, medium of exchange, and unit of account. The

---

[181] FRED, "Deposits, All Commercial Banks; Currency in Circulation."
[182] Scott Pelley, "Fed Chair Jerome Powell's *60 Minutes* Interview,"
[183] Luke Broyles, "We Are Living in the Ancient World and Bitcoin is Going to Kill It."

weaponization of the US dollar via sanctions severely diminishes other countries' perception that our fiat fills these historical properties of money. Now that there is little barrier for other countries to print their own without doing any real work (ie, backing it by gold or some other protocol requiring an expenditure of energy), the perception of scarcity that fiat once had has vanished.

Despite all the shortcomings of fiat, it is still the most widely used form of value transfer. This may be due to a multitude of reasons. Some might choose to not see fiat's drawbacks due to a "we've always done it that way" mentality. Many in society could be stuck in a high time preference/poverty mindset where they don't have the bandwidth to perceive potential systemic upgrades. Others benefit more from this fiat system thanks to the Cantillon Effect. Named after eighteenth-century Irish-French economist Richard Cantillon, the Cantillon Effect suggests those who are closer to the supply of money (generally those politically connected) when newly minted benefit more than those who receive it later or last.[184]

Fiat's credibility as a scarce asset has deteriorated since its inception. The US dollar has reportedly lost 97% of its purchasing power since 1913.[185] The fun thing with math is that this trend can keep going; it can still (and probably continue to) drop for all eternity. It will do so because the fiduciaries responsible for maintaining the public's faith in fiat have bastardized one of its main use cases. Confoundingly, it's still widely used. Guess we should all aspire to be politically connected. What a world that would be [sarcasm indeed implied].

---

[184] Arkadiusz Sieroń, *Money, Inflation and Business Cycles: The Cantillon Effect and the Economy.*
[185] FRED, "Consumer Price Index for All Urban Consumers: Purchasing Power of the Consumer Dollar in U.S. City Average."

"Crypto" (Altcoins, Stablecoins & CBDCs)

Although bitcoin has technically and historically been considered a cryptocurrency, for the purpose of this section, we will refer to the word "crypto" as any digital asset not named bitcoin that utilizes blockchain technology, is decentralized in name only (DINO), with the intent to enrich its founders. All cryptos, alternative coins (altcoins), stablecoins, and central bank digital currencies (CBDCs) have a central issuer. This means that the humans in control, with all their fallible desires, have the ability to change the supply of their coin at will, which immediately degrades its credibility. Upon launch of their project, all founders have the ability to "premine" their token. This means they can allocate a predetermined amount of their supply to whoever they want (usually initial large investors). As discussed in the section on fiat, this allows the Cantillon Effect to take place; those closest to the money spigot benefit while the people further away suffer. These inherent conflicts of interest are known as the *agency problem*.

Another consideration when determining the scarcity of crypto is realizing how easy it is to replicate. With technological developments ever-increasing, one can copy the code of a crypto and create their own within minutes. The barrier to entry is low, even if an aspiring altcoin creator doesn't have the requisite knowledge to do so. Blockchain-as-a-service (BaaS) is a service that allows people to build projects with cloud-based solutions. With this ability, the value proposition derived from scarcity is greatly diminished.

Stablecoins are designed to have relatively stable prices. This is accomplished by attempting to peg its crypto to a commodity, currency, or a basket of assets. Some even attempt to regulate their supply by using algorithms. Regardless of their individual composition, there is still a group of individuals able to change its supply. In times of stress, the controllers of the code can easily succumb to external pressures. Recent years have shown many stablecoins to be anything but *stable*.

Although the following is not particularly an aspect related to scarcity, it is important to point out that when governments begin dabbling in crypto (CBDCs), all the aforementioned negatives of fiat and crypto are packaged together with all the negatives of a surveillance state. For example, China's digital yuan has implemented multiple measures to limit their constituents' freedoms and privacy while promoting the Communist Party of China's brand of social engineering. Saying something the government doesn't like could get citizens' accounts frozen or emptied.[186] The authorities can add an expiration date to force you to spend, which would force the mindset of high time preference upon its citizens.

In an article for *Bitcoin Magazine*, Chief Strategy Officer at the Human Rights Foundation, Alex Gladstein, argued that China's CBDC is a "tool for surveillance and social engineering."[187] Gladstein also warned that China's digital currency push could have global implications, particularly if other countries follow suit. In a tweet from November 2020, he said: "As we can see from China, surveillance

---

[186] James Dorn, "China's Digital Yuan: A Threat to Freedom."
[187] Alex Gladstein, "In China, It's Blockchain and Tyranny Vs. Bitcoin and Freedom."
IN CHINA, IT'S BLOCKCHAIN AND TYRANNY VS BITCOIN AND FREEDOM

---

fintech can be used in the service of tyranny. The CCP is harnessing mobile payments to create an Orwellian surveillance state and launch massive social engineering projects. The Chinese CBDC, called DC/EP, is already being rolled out."[188] Scarcity would be the least of worries for citizens under a CBDC. It's not money; it's a social credit system. So they've created an asset with, at best, an undetermined amount of scarcity with the ability for mass surveillance and control. Cool...

---

[188] Alex Gladstein, "As We Can See From China..."

Bitcoin

Created in 2008 by Satoshi Nakamoto, Bitcoin represents the benefits of all previously mentioned assets while also being the most scarce on the planet. Written into its code is a terminal limit of no more than twenty-one million coins, each divisible to the eighth decimal place. It is important to note that, thanks to it being the only truly decentralized protocol, it is nearly impossible to change the code. Sure, someone could come along and make their own version (called a "fork"), but then that version does not inherit the properties of Bitcoin; it becomes a centralized altcoin with all the drawbacks mentioned in previous sections.

Bitcoin's scarcity is what led people to consider it "digital gold." Similar to gold, the stock-to-flow of bitcoin is very high; it has a large existing stock (over 19M coins) relative to its annual production (currently 6.25 coins roughly every ten minutes). This amount gets cut in half every four years in what is known as the "halving." Where gold miners can crank up the machines when the price of gold goes up, Bitcoin's protocol follows the rules set forth since inception without fail regardless of exchange rate fluctuations. This inflexibility, scheduled tightening of incoming supply, along with steadily increasing demand is primarily why society has seen large spikes in bitcoin's exchange rate price (the exchange rate can also be seen as the value of the dollar decreasing dramatically versus the price of bitcoin).

As long as we have a civilization, we will continue to produce goods and services. Having the most overwhelmingly scarce asset to serve as a unit of measurement means that the prices of goods and services will decrease over time as more is added to our economy. This is a hard concept to grasp for most. Most of the people living today have been conditioned to rising prices due to inflationary monetary policies. We've grown accustomed to "inflation-adjusted" numbers. As Knut Svanholm points out, when we transition to live on a Bitcoin standard, "everything [will be] divided by twenty-one million."[189] Having an asset that provides absolute scarcity allows us to all use the same measuring stick to measure value consistently across time for eternity.

Some of Bitcoin's detractors point to its scarcity as a drawback. The thought goes... there won't be enough for everyone to use it as money; in times of economic contraction, the liquidity will dry up. This couldn't be further from the truth. While the current fiat system solves the liquidity issue with massive and increasing amounts of dollars, this system results in persistent inflation. Fiat's solution is to add places (dollars) to the left of the decimal point. With the digital nature of bitcoin, it is infinitely divisible; we can add an unlimited amount of places to the right of the decimal point. For the first time in history, we have a system that provides absolute scarcity while also providing unlimited liquidity.

As Heritage Foundation economist and Mises Institute fellow Professor Peter St. Onge explained to me in proper Austrian economic thought, "The price of bitcoin simply adjusts to whatever liquidity the bitcoin market needs (i.e., twice the demand means twice the price, hence as if there was twice as much bitcoin circulating). As for the

---

[189] Knut Svanholm, *Bitcoin: Everything Divided by 21 Million.*

question whether people just HODL (Bitcoin parlance for "hold") all the bitcoin in times of distress, this is also true for gold historically, and it simply means deflation happens fast (i.e. gold price goes up fast) then things normalize again."[190]

All things considered, bitcoin's absolute scarcity represents a paradigm shift. It is one of the main reasons why many cannot wrap their heads around its value proposition. Every scarce asset up to this point has represented relative scarcity, which society has valued over less scarce assets. With Bitcoin being both a network (uppercase "B") *and* an asset (lowercase "b"), the value proposition is affected not only by its absolute scarcity but also its network effects. Metcalfe's Law states that a network's impact is the square of the number of nodes in the network. Please take time to consider the following complementary factors… Bitcoin the network is growing exponentially (faster than the adoption of the internet) while bitcoin the asset is reducing in issuance (incoming supply cut in half every four years; known as the "halving") with a terminal supply limit of 21 million coins. Once the interplay of these two factors clicks for you, you'll start to grasp its true value potential.

---

[190] Peter St. Onge, personal correspondence with the author.

Scarcity

"Abundance in money = scarcity everywhere else…
scarcity in money = abundance everywhere else."[191]
~ Jeff Booth

Scarce things tend to better hold value over time than abundant things. Scarcity creates a situation where the supply of a particular resource or asset is limited, while demand remains high. This results in higher prices and greater value for the resource or asset, as people are willing to pay more to obtain it.

Scarcity also implies that the resource or asset is difficult to produce or obtain, which can make it more desirable and sought after. Being able to create assets without having expended energy (or capital) in some form results in an asset that is easily replicable, which results in it losing its property of scarcity. When the cost of capital is zero, the worth of that capital is also zero.

Fiat and "crypto" (altcoins, stablecoins, and CBDCs) are not scarce due to the factors previously listed. Also add the fact that these are permissioned, centralized, mutable, and require trust, and their value decreases relative to bitcoin. While gold is relatively scarce, it too suffers from the ability to be confiscated (Executive Order 6102) as well as the requirement of trust on behalf of the custodian.

In my opinion, time is our most scarce asset. Unless we become the society portrayed in the 2011 science fiction action film, *In Time*, where "Once your time runs out, you die," we will not be able to spend or trade our time as an asset; in reality, time is not a directly exchangeable asset. This is why we have an intermediary, namely what we call money; one of money's main functions is store of value. Since we can't directly trade time, we have solved this by using whatever is the best store of value of each era. The era we've entered has brought us bitcoin,

---

[191] Jeff Booth, "Abundance in Money = Scarcity Everywhere Else."

which is the most scarce asset history has ever seen. I believe bitcoin gives us the ability to store our time and effort better than anything else.

Conclusion

"Necessity is the mother of invention."
~ Anonymous

Bitcoin, more specifically, the properties of Bitcoin have always been with us. It just took humanity centuries to realize the worth of each property individually and then build the infrastructure well enough to realize them collectively, which many believe is Bitcoin. When all the examined properties are able to meld into a single monetary unit in cyberspace, a digital representation of virtuous guardrails emerge. When all properties are able to act harmoniously in a digital, global monetary network, the societal benefits are as limitless as our collective imagination.

Humans will be more easily able to evolve and move past the errors of the past. If the opportunity to learn from mistakes is taken away, the same mistakes will keep getting made. As a society, we now have that ability to show we've done the work to learn from our collective mistakes by interacting in a voluntary system where there are no rulers, only rules (hence the Bitcoin quip *rules without rulers*).Even more so, similar to the Golden Rule, Bitcoin's set of rules are relatively few when compared to the myriad set of rules in and between current global monetary systems (US dollar, SWIFT, China's digital yuan, etc.).

Former Apple CEO, Steve Jobs once said, "It was impossible to connect the dots looking forward when I was in college. But it was very, very clear looking backwards ten years later."[192] The essence of Jobs' quote was the impetus for this book. The episodes portrayed in this book are only a fraction of the possible lessons we can learn from history. Let us take a moment to summarize the information we've

---

[192] Steve Jobs, "Stanford Commencement Address," 7.

covered and synthesize this knowledge into a deeper understanding of Bitcoin.

Permissionlessness

As history has taught us, the propagation of permissionless systems over time has offered communities an ability to better express their values in a peaceful and voluntary manner. The Protestant Reformation allowed for individual spiritual empowerment. The fight against Jim Crow laws signified a continued desire for individuals to live free of oppressive, immoral laws. Executive Order 6102 showed us that with too much power comes the ability to overreach and control humans' ability to store their own wealth the way they see fit. The Berlin Wall shows a similar theme to EO6102 in that the powerful will inevitably restrict the powerless, even in their ability to move freely. I would bet that, after considering the comparisons in the section *A Tale of Two Koreas*, most, if not all, people would choose to live in the less permissioned South Korea. These are only a few of the multitude of examples throughout history that show the value of adopting permissionless systems.

Bitcoin is permissionless, meaning that anyone is able to participate in the Bitcoin network without requiring authorization from an authority. Anyone with access to the internet and a smartphone can participate in the network without permission. Bitcoin does not discriminate on the basis of race, gender, age, nationality, or religion. Bitcoin is for everyone. There is no intermediary or third party. The Bitcoin network distributes the shared ledger of transactions across nodes — computers running the same protocol. Anyone and everyone can participate without permission.

Contrast this against our legacy financial system, which is permissioned to the point where roughly 1.7 billion adults remain unbanked.[193] This is partly due to the unnecessary bureaucratic process to access financial services. It's also due to the former lack of a permissionless global settlement layer. Approximately 70% of El Salvador's population was unbanked prior to their adoption of Bitcoin

---

[193] World Bank, "Financial Inclusion."

as legal tender.[194] This was one of the motivating factors for the decision to embrace a Bitcoin standard.

Bitcoin's permissionless nature allows for greater financial freedom. It promotes inclusivity. It's voluntary, which is in stark contrast to the coercive systems in which we currently live. Thanks to Bitcoin, humanity is enabled to participate free of permission in pursuing their version of life, liberty, and pursuit of happiness on a global scale.

---

[194] David Coker, "Bitcoin: El Salvador's Grand Experiment."

Gaining Consensus

Good ideas don't require force. This shouldn't be a controversial thought, but it seems as though, in today's society, it is. If you feel for Ignaz Semmelweis' predicament or respect the method implemented by the Grand Council of the Six Nations, you can see the benefit from gaining consensus. If you see the follies in the Munich Agreement or the harmony in the Good Friday Agreement, you know proper consensus can be achieved through systems that consider human incentives. Solving the Byzantine Generals Problem proved this to be true.

Bitcoin is able to gain consensus through proof-of-work, which is a process that ensures all participants in the network agree on the validity of each transaction and help maintain the security of the system. As previously mentioned, all of this is voluntary. It is critically important to stress this point because true consensus flourishes in voluntary systems. This is in stark opposition to coercive systems in which individuals are forced to comply with rules and regulations under threat of punishment.

As long as we have a democratic spirit inside us, we have to see the value in a global network able to consistently and repeatedly gain true consensus for eternity. Many Bitcoiners aren't buying bitcoin for short-term gain; they are buying for future generations. Choosing between fiat and bitcoin is like choosing between patching up a cracked and faulty foundation or getting a new and improved foundation capable of lasting in perpetuity. Imagine the quality of potential human interactions when consensus is reached in this fashion.

Decentralization

If you've ever watched birds fly in their beautiful but seemingly meandering patterns, you've seen nature utilizing the property of decentralization with behavior known as "self-organization." They do this by observing the movements of the birds closest to them and adjusting their own movements accordingly. No one central bird is in charge, yet the flock coordinates their movements through independent observation and adjustment.

We've hopefully learned from the effects of overcentralization of power in action with the fall of the Western Roman Empire as well as the fall of the Soviet Union. We've witnessed the opening of the floodgates of knowledge from the invention of the printing press. We've grasped that governments can thrive despite being sufficiently decentralized. We've lived through the internet and all the ways in which it enhanced our lives.

Bitcoin is decentralized thanks to its ledger being distributed among tens of thousands of nodes. There's no need for a central authority to validate and process transactions. This is beneficial to all network participants because even if many nodes go down or are hacked, the network can continue to operate. This also means that no one, regardless of their perceived power, can change the rules of Bitcoin or game the system for their own benefit.

Thanks to Bitcoin's consensus mechanism, the agreement of the majority of the nodes ensures a fair and transparent system for all users. Thanks to its decentralization, the Bitcoin network is resistant to censorship, its data is free from immutability, and the asset is void of internal manipulation.

Trust Minimization

While trust is a critical factor in relationships, accepting the fact that humans are fallible and prone to opportunism is a prerequisite to understanding why we should continue to promote trustless systems. Victor Lustig and Charles Ponzi taught us the extent to which humans can't be trusted as well as how naive we can actually be. We've observed how easily the trust of a citizenry can be manipulated by fractional reserve banking. We've gained respect for the efforts of the Navajo Code Talkers' ability to create creative trust minimized systems. We've developed the ability to further perfect trustlessness with the advent of the Gold Codes.

Bitcoin represents the property of trust minimization through the melding of its other properties such as decentralization, consensus mechanism, and immutability. Because Bitcoin is decentralized, there is less need to trust any individual node to not change the protocol's rules. It is from this where we get the well-known phrase in Bitcoin, "don't trust, verify." Thanks to Bitcoin's proof-of-work consensus mechanism and its necessary energy expenditure, we are ensured the network is secure as it is currently more powerful than the top 500 supercomputers combined.[195] Bitcoin's immutability ensures that all transactions are irreversible, which makes it impossible to cheat the system. Add in the fact that Bitcoin transactions are pseudonymous, addresses are not tied to real identities, and we have the most trust-minimized, international system of transacting value the world has ever seen.

When a house of cards is built, most people understand all it takes is a gust of wind to topple it down. When we build systems that require trust upon a monetary system that requires trust, how do we not see the possibility for a similar conclusion? The systemic risk in our current

---

[195] Maria Santos, "Not Even the Top 500 Supercomputers Combined Are More Powerful Than the Bitcoin Network."

system is apparently clear to anyone with a discerning eye. We must trust that our money won't be corrupted by the system conductors who benefit from the corruption. We must trust they won't debase our wealth despite decades of proof to the contrary. We must trust that all the businesses and organizations built on this system will stand strong in the face of a gust of wind.

Bitcoin's properties work in concert in order to make a secure and trust-minimized system. It is internally resistant to manipulation and fraud. No further do we need to stand on the faulty, easily exploited foundations of the past. We now have a new way for financial realization with a system that is transparent and fair, free from the need of trusted middlemen and rent-seekers. It's ironic how the implementation of trustless systems has the ability to increase trust in other aspects of society.

Censorship Resistance

Societies who value censorship resistance are societies that bear its fruits, namely freedom of speech, financial freedom, innovation, and respect for privacy. Socrates and Edward Snowden gave us blueprints for how to morally stand up to unchecked authority. The Samizdat and the Arab Spring gave us viable workarounds against oppressive regimes. The Great Firewall of China shows us what the future will look like if we don't stand for our rights and instead allow the continuous creep of communist controls.

Bitcoin is incorruptible and uncensorable information. This is all possible thanks to the aforementioned properties of decentralization, permissionlessness, immutability, etc. If you consider, like I do, how people spend their money as a form of speech, then Bitcoin represents the most powerful tool for resisting censorship. Simply by owning bitcoin (provided you are the custodian), you are not only expressing your right to speech, you are also potentially supporting the financial freedom of eight billion people.

The opposite of this is institutionalized paternalism whereby limits are placed on our autonomy in order for a select few to promote their version of the greater good. As Benjamin Franklin said "Those who would give up essential liberty, to purchase a little temporary safety, deserve neither liberty nor safety."[196] By outsourcing our financial freedom in the name of security, we are tacitly outsourcing our right to liberty. Thomas Sowell famously said, "There are no solutions; there are only trade-offs."[197] I believe this is not a trade-off that we should make as a society because the second- and third-order effects potentially lead to a dystopian world void of natural human rights.

In a vacuum, most people would value empowerment over oppression. So why not utilize a tool that embodies this? Bitcoin

---

[196] Benjamin Franklin, "Pennsylvania Assembly: Reply to the Governor."

[197] Thomas Sowell, *The Vision of the Anointed*, 142.

empowers not only individuals, but the world to express financial freedom as well as freedom of speech.

Open Source Collaboration

Embracing the spirit of open source collaboration allows for greater transparency and accountability — whether it be at the public level as with Liechtenstein or at the private level with the GNU project, Linux, Khan Academy, or Wikipedia. Following the lead of visionaries like Richard M. Stallman, Linus Torvaldis, Sal Khan, Jimmy Wales, we can continue forward into history's unwritten chapters with the assuredness that we can build better systems when collaboration is prioritized over proprietorship.

The antithesis of open source is closed source. These include proprietary systems and walled gardens that in essence cut off the potential for natural human collaboration. Taken to its extreme, closed source systems can lead to dystopian societies. Take for example *The Matrix*. In that movie, the artificial intelligence system was completely closed, with no way for humans to access or modify its underlying code. Because of this opaqueness, it was a powerful tool used to control and enslave humanity. Having no understanding of the system or being able to modify the system led to citizens inside being unaware of their own slavery. The lack of transparency can be an oppressive tool. If Bitcoin represents freedom, what does the class of the entitled, politically connected attempting to ban Bitcoin represent?

Bitcoin's software is open source, which means that anyone can access the code and contribute to its development. This collaborative approach to building and improving upon Bitcoin's protocol is paramount to a society that values inclusivity. Thanks to Bitcoin's public ledger, everyone can access and review its code. Thanks to its strong community of developers, users, and enthusiasts, Bitcoin creates a level playing field of participation where anyone can contribute. Open source software is essential for creating a fair and transparent financial system that is accessible to everyone.

Immutability

While not everything needs to be stored for time immemorial (I'm thinking of every time I've sent a poop emoji), some things such as financial transactions might be of some societal use to record. History has echoed our desire to document what we find valuable. We've been doing this at least since early humans drew petroglyphs on cave walls. The Ten Commandments showed us that, regardless of the medium used, moral code can stand the test of time. Newton's Laws of motion showed us that, while the understanding of science is always developing, certain fundamental laws cannot be changed even if a few disagree. The Watergate scandal showed us that no one is above immutability. And an ongoing unfortunate lesson learned from Julian Assange's story is that we should embrace, not reject, those who shine light on the immutable truth.

What's the opposite, though? Something that is mutable or alterable? Sure, there's times I wish children would know when it's socially appropriate to turn their voices off, but I'm not in favor of changing their very nature. Trying to shut the other person up or change the facts of an argument is something children do. The fact that we allow adults to do this at the highest level of society, and with our money nonetheless, is absurd. Money should be a tool for annotating voluntary transactions, not for manipulation or control.

Bitcoin is a powerful tool for financial transactions and record-keeping. Once a transaction is recorded on Bitcoin's blockchain, it cannot be altered or deleted. The record of the transaction is permanent and immutable. This creates a high degree of certainty and trust in the system, which is essential for it to be used as a reliable form of money. Implementing these concepts of transparency, security, and efficiency into our global monetary system should be a no-brainer.

Scarcity

I remember back to my childhood playing video games. The games in which I had unlimited lives were the games I displayed the most reckless behavior. I believe that was the case because they weren't scarce. Scarcity is not a new phenomenon. We've been grappling with the scarcity of time for as long as we've been aware of it. We've been valuing gold since ancient civilizations realized its scarcity; we've been disrespecting scarcity ever since the inception of fiat money. We've doubled down on that disrespect with the advent of "crypto" and CBDCs. It's time to return to the reality that scarcity warrants our respect.

If Bitcoin embodies production before consumption, fiat, "crypto," and CBDCs embody consumption before production. Traditional finance has become a real-life game of musical chairs, but with the guise that we'll be given a chair at the end of the game. Sure, you can have credit on a debt-based system, but at what price? The exponential rise in fiat money supply, the massive amounts of political currency units being shipped to other countries, and the insurmountable amount of debt being hand-waved away should cause some level of alarm in the average citizen. What happens to the fiat value of what you own when the music stops?

There can never be more than 21 million bitcoin in existence. This limit is hard-coded into the Bitcoin protocol. This limit is intended to prevent inflation and ensure that bitcoin retains its value over time. Bitcoiners have a phrase that goes "1 BTC = 1 BTC." This shows the intrinsic value of bitcoin in that its value is not subject to fiat fluctuations or other external factors. In addition, because of Bitcoin's halving schedule, the incoming supply becomes progressively more scarce over time.

The specter of scarcity looms large over each of us, whether one is aware of it or not. It is up to us to collectively respect that. The scarcity of bitcoin protects us from the ills of short-term, low time preference greed of the power-hungry elitists. We can attain abundance through the acceptance of scarcity.

History Echoes Bitcoin

*"Those who cannot remember the past are condemned to repeat it."*198

~ George Santayana

Please notice how little of this book has been about price or exchange rate. That is on purpose because my perception has been that most *normies'* — the affectionate nickname Bitcoiners have for the average citizen yet to gain these realizations — knowledge of the exchange rate somehow translates to comprehension of the protocol and its potential societal benefits. This couldn't be further from the truth. The volatility you see in bitcoin's price is a function of many things, including the asymmetry of understanding regarding this once-in-a-generation discovery/invention. It can be argued that, while the US dollar exchange rate of bitcoin the asset has been volatile, Bitcoin the protocol is the exact opposite; it is predictable with blocks produced roughly every ten minutes and a code verifiable to all. These assurances and more are what lead Bitcoiners to say "tick tock, next block."

Let's continue this with a thought experiment. Let's pretend there's no price to bitcoin; it's a static price. You still have the ability to choose and interact between the fiat network and the Bitcoin network. Which one would you choose? Based on all the previous chapters, consider the following… you can choose fiat, a permissioned, centralized, highly censored, closed source, mutable system, which requires a massive amount of trust (even though you're coerced to use it), and it has an unlimited and erratic supply. On the other hand, you have Bitcoin, which is a permissionless, decentralized, trustless, censorship resistant, open source, immutable consensus mechanism with the most scarce asset ever discovered/invented. In light of this characterization, how is this a hard decision? I know which one I choose to own and hold.

---

198 George Santayana, *The Life of Reason,* 284.

The physical act of purchasing bitcoin is not the pinnacle of virtue. If you want to capture the entire value that Bitcoin offers, you need to show the mental proof of work required to comprehend at least a fraction of what this invention can do. Most of your normie friends won't, though. Everyone will have their reasons and justifications. Some will go back to their bread and circuses. Most will lose focus in order to support "the next thing." Some of your friends will become butthurt because they think they missed out (even though they haven't). Many will continue believing that the solution to life's ills can be solved through subjugating their will to an equally flawed human (even though history tells a different story). Some will remain intellectually dishonest (despite that never being a valid long-term strategy). Some will get stuck in high time preference altcoin scams and feel the need to attack bitcoin (in spite of the overwhelming evidence to the contrary). History will be the final judge, as it has always been.

When you hear Bitcoiners say "fix the money, fix the world" or "Bitcoin fixes this," please understand this is not some marketing ploy. Bitcoiners have been poking holes, finding attack vectors, and being adversarial, in order to verify that this is indeed the most robust and antifragile protocol discovered/invented to date. It comes from a place of sincerity and, well, proof of work. Most people inside the Bitcoin industry have spent countless hours understanding both the problem and how Bitcoin is the solution. We're fed up with generations not learning the lessons of their ancestors, especially in terms of manipulation of money. Fixing these inefficiencies in nature is called evolution. We know history has been sussing this out in an iterative pattern for as long as we have recorded.

If any of this resonates in you, please reach out to local Bitcoin meetups for support, listen to podcasts, read other Bitcoin books, keep an open mind, do the work, donate to developers, and realize Bitcoiners are attempting to build the world in which we want to live. These properties all have some level of value to society. Together they have the potential to create a prosperous and morally superior society. History has proven the value of these individual properties time and again. It is time for us to collectively realize these properties can all be achieved synergistically with Bitcoin. Understanding how the properties inherent in money we choose changes individuals' incentive structure is the first step to understanding why Bitcoin is the best form of money.

If you enjoyed this book, please consider purchasing one for a family member or a friend, leave a review, or make a donation!

References

Allen, Robert C. "The Rise and Decline of the Soviet Economy," *Canadian Journal of Economics* 34, 4 (2001): 859–881.

Ammous, Saifedean. *The Fiat: The Debt Slavery Alternative to Human Civilization.* The Saif House, 2021.

Applebaum, Anne. *Red Famine: Stalin's War on Ukraine.* Doubleday: New York, 2017.

Aronczyk, Melissa. "Brands and the Pandemic: A Cautionary Tale," *Social Media + Society* July-September (2020): 1–4.

Assange, Julian. *Cypherpunks: Freedom and the Future of the Internet.* OR Books: New York, 2012.

Axelrod, Robert. *The Evolution of Cooperation.* New York: Basic Books, 1984.

Ayres, Robert U. *The History and Future of Technology: Can Technology Save Humanity From Extinction?* Springer: Cham, Switzerland, 2021.

Becker, S. O., Praff, Rubin, Jared. "Causes and consequences of the Protestant Reformation." *Explorations in Economic History* 62 (2016): 1–25.

Bednarik, Robert G. "The Technology of Petroglyphs," *Rock Art Research* 15, 1 (1998): 23–35.

Bernstein, Carl and Woodward, Bob. *All the President's Men.* Simon & Schuster: New York, 1974.

Bernstein, William J. *The Delusions of Crowds: Why People Go Mad in Groups.* New York: Grove Atlantic, 2021.

Bird, Douglas W. and Bird, Rebecca Bliege. "Signalling Theory and Durable Symbolic Expression." In *The Oxford Handbook of the Archeology and Anthropology of Rock Art*, edited by Bruno David and Ian J. McNiven, 343–361. Oxford University Press: New York, 2018.

Booth, Jeff. "Abundance in Money = Scarcity Everywhere Else." *Twitter*. July 2, 2022: https://twitter.com/JeffBooth/status/1543291963117473792

Booth, Jeff. "Finding Signal in a Noisy World." *Bitcoin Magazine* September 9, 2022: https://bitcoinmagazine.com/culture/bitcoin-signal-in-this-noisy-world

Breedlove, Robert. "Immutable Money Permanently Unmutes the Voice of the People." *Twitter* February 23, 2021: https://twitter.com/breedlove22/status/1364258111133949953?s=46&t=e21sQiGkj8Vk-5Yvov0jdA

Broyles, Luke. "We Are Living in the Ancient World and Bitcoin is Going to Kill It." *Citadel 21* vol 20. January 21, 2023: https://www.citadel21.com/we-are-living-in-the-ancient-world-and-bitcoin-is-going-to-kill-it

Brunton, Finn. *Digital Cash: The Unknown History of the Anarchists, Utopians, and Technologists who Created Cryptocurrency.* Princeton, N.J.: Princeton University Press, 2019.

Bukovsky, Vladimir. *To Build a Castle: My Life as a Dissenter.* Andre Deutsch; First Edition, translated by Michael Scammell.

Cambridge Centre for Alternative Finance. "Bitcoin Network Power Demand." Accessed May 1, 2023: https://ccaf.io/cbnsi/cbeci

Carter, K. Codell and Carter, Barbara R. *Childbed Fever: A Scientific Biography of Ignaz Semmelweis.* Abingdon, Oxon: Routledge, 2017.

Casebourne, Imogen. Davies, Chris, Fernandes, Michelle and Norman Naomi. "Assessing the Accuracy and Quality of Wikipedia Entries Compared to Popular Online Encyclopaedias: A Comparative Preliminary Study Across Disciplines in English, Spanish and Arabic." Epic and University of Oxford, UK, 2012.

Chan, Chi Ling. "Fallen Behind: Science, Technology, and Soviet Statism," *Intersect: The Stanford Journal of Science, Technology, and Society* 8, 3 (2015): 1–11.

Chaum, David L. "Blind Signatures for Untraceable Payments," *Advances in Cryptology* 83 (1983): 153–159.

Chaum, David L. "Untraceable Electronic Mail, Return Addresses, and Digital Pseudonyms," *Communications of the ACM* 24, 2 (1981): 84–90.

Chawaga, Peter. "Free Assange: Inside a Cypherpunk's Fight to Publish the Secrets of Superpowers." *Bitcoin Magazine*, Gatekeeper's issue (May 2023): 14–31.

Chepenik, Conor. Personal correspondence with the author, May 10, 2023.

Cho, Adrian. "Can Dark Matter Vanquish a Rival Theory?" *Science*. January 25, 2017: https://www.science.org/content/article/can-dark-matter-vanquish-rival-theory

Church, Clive and Head, Randolph. *A Concise History of Switzerland.* Cambridge University Press: New York, 2013.

Churchill, Winston. "The Munich Agreement: October 5, 1938. House of Commons." International Churchill Society. Available via: https://winstonchurchill.org/resources/speeches/1930-1938-the-wilderness/the-munich-agreement/

CNN. "Prince wins Liechtenstein Powers." March 16, 2003: https://edition.cnn.com/2003/WORLD/europe/03/16/liechtenstein.reut/index.html

Coker, David. "Bitcoin: El Salvador's Grand Experiment." *The Conversation.* June 9, 2021: https://theconversation.com/bitcoin-el-salvadors-grand-experiment-162382

Colitt, Leslie. "Escape from East Berlin." *The Guardian.* August 16, 2011: https://www.theguardian.com/world/2011/aug/16/escape-from-east-berlin

Colon, Christóbal. "The Fourth Voyage of Columbus." in *The Northmen, Columbus, and Cabot, 985-1503: The Voyages of the Northmen. The Voyages of Columbus and of John Cabot.* Charles Scribner's Sons: New York, 1906. Available online via Project Gutenberg: https://gutenberg.org/files/18571/18571-h/18571-h.htm#Solomon

Crabbe, Leland. "The International Gold Standard and US Monetary Policy from World War I to the New Deal," *Federal Reserve Bulletin*, June (1989): 423–440.

Creemers, Rogier. "Internet Information Service Management Measures." Digichina, at Stanford University. September 25, 2000: https://digichina.stanford.edu/work/internet-information-service-management-rules/

Darby, Mary. "In Ponzi We Trust." *The Smithsonian Magazine,* December 1998: https://www.smithsonianmag.com/history/in-ponzi-we-trust-64016168/

Davies, Dave. "Journalist Who Helped Break Snowden's Story Reflects On His High-Stakes Reporting." NPR. May 20, 2020: https://www.npr.org/2020/05/20/859376407/journalist-who-helped-break-snowdens-story-reflects-on-his-high-stakes-reporting

Dawson, Graham, Dover, Jo, and Hopkins, Stephen. *The Northern Ireland Troubles in Britain: Impacts, Engagements, Legacies and Memories.* Manchester University Press: Manchester, 2017.

Dictionary.com. "Permission." Accessed May 1, 2023: https://www.dictionary.com/browse/permission

Diem, Aubrey, Egli, Emil, Maissen, Thomas, and Wachter, Daniel. "Switzerland: Government and Society." Encyclopædia Britannica, last updated January 3, 2023: https://www.britannica.com/place/Switzerland/Government-and-society

Donough, Frank. *Neville Chamberlain, Appeasement, and the British Road to War.* Manchester University Press: Manchester, UK.

Donvan, John. "President Bill Clinton Lost Nuclear Codes While in Office, New Book Claims." *ABC News.* October 21, 2010: https://abcnews.go.com/WN/president-bill-clinton-lost-nuclear-codes-office-book/story?id=11930878

Dorn, James A. "China's Digital Yuan: A Threat to Freedom." Cato At Liberty, Cato Blog, August 25, 2021: https://www.cato.org/blog/chinas-digital-yuan-threat-freedom

Duignan, Brian. "Ten Commandments." *Encyclopædia Britannica.*
November 20, 2020: https://www.britannica.com/topic/Ten-Commandments

Dunn, Donald. *Ponzi: The Incredible True Story of the King of Financial Cons.* Broadway Books: New York, 2005.

Durrett, Deanne. *Unsung Heroes of World War II.* University of Nebraska Press: Lincoln, NE., 2009.

Eccles, Marriner S. "Federal Reserve Act Amendment: Hearings before the Committee on Banking and Currency, House of Representatives, 78th Congress, 1st Session, H.R. 1699." Government Printing Office, Washington 1943.

Eichengreen, Barry. *Golden Fetters: The Gold Standard and the Great Depression, 1919–1939.* New York: Oxford University Press, 1995.

Eisenstein, Elizabeth L. *The Printing Press as an Agent of Change.* Cambridge University Press: Cambridge, UK, 1980.

Federal Reserve Economic Data. "Consumer Price Index for All Urban Consumers: Purchasing Power of the Consumer Dollar in U.S. City Average." FRED database, accessed May 8, 2023: https://fred.stlouisfed.org/graph/?g=12CZr

Federal Reserve Economic Data. "Deposits, All Commercial Banks; Currency in Circulation." FRED database, accessed May 8, 2023: https://fred.stlouisfed.org/graph/?g=13iOb

Finney, Hal. "RPOW - Reusable Proofs of Work," Satoshi Nakamoto Institute. August 15, 2004. https://nakamotoinstitute.org/rpow/

Foo, Alvin. "'Nearly Every War That Has Started in the Last 50 Years Have Been a Result of Media Lies.' - Julian Assange." Twitter. August 31, 2022: https://twitter.com/alvinfoo/status/1565082125321359366

Franklin, Benjamin. "Advice to a Young Tradesman." In *The American Instructor: Or Young Man's Best Companion*, 9th edition. Edited by George Fisher: 375–7. New Printing Office: Philadelphia, 1748 (Yale University Library).

Franklin, Benjamin. "Pennsylvania Assembly: Reply to the Governor." In *Votes and Proceedings of the House of Representatives*, 1755–1756: 19–21. Philadelphia, 1756. Available online via National Archives: https://founders.archives.gov/documents/Franklin/01-06-02-0107

Free Software Foundation. "What is Free Software?" June 25, 2022: https://www.gnu.org/philosophy/free-sw.en.html

Freedom House. "Freedom in the World 2023, 50th Anniversary Edition." March 2023, available via: https://freedomhouse.org/sites/default/files/2023-03/FIW_World_2023_DigtalPDF.pdf

Freedom House. "Freedom in the World 2023: China." March 2023, available via: https://freedomhouse.org/country/china/freedom-world/2023

Frost, Robert. "The Road Not Taken." Poetry Foundation: https://www.poetryfoundation.org/poems/44272/the-road-not-taken

Gandhi, Mahatma. *All Men Are Brothers*. Columbia University Press: New York, 1953.

Garrick-Mason, Ian. "Why Rome Fell." *The Spectator* August 27, 2005: https://www.spectator.co.uk/article/why-rome-fell/

Giles, Jim. "Internet Encyclopaedias Go Head to Head," *Nature* 438 (2005): 900–901.

Gladstein, Alex. "As We Can See China…" Twitter, November 17, 2020: https://twitter.com/gladstein/status/1328772065290113024

Gladstein, Alex. "In China, It's Blockchain and Tyranny Vs. Bitcoin and Freedom." *Bitcoin Magazine*, September 21, 2021: https://bitcoinmagazine.com/culture/op-ed-in-china-its-blockchain-and-tyranny-vs-bitcoin-and-freedom

Goldstein, Jacob. *Money: The True Story of a Made-Up Thing*. Hachette: New York, 2020.

Griffin, G. Edward. *The Creature from Jekyll Island*. American Media: Westlake Village, CA., 2002.

Guarino, Ben. "The Oldest Story Ever Told is Painted on This Cave Wall, Archaeologists Report." *Washington Post*. December 11, 2019:
https://www.washingtonpost.com/science/2019/12/11/oldest-story-ever-told-is-painted-this-cave-wall-archaeologists-report/

Guesmi, Haythem. "The Social Media Myth About the Arab Spring." *Al Jazeera*. January 27, 2021:
https://www.aljazeera.com/opinions/2021/1/27/the-social-media-myth-about-the-arab-spring

Gunter, Jill. "Crypto's Bad Incentives Are Dying." *Financial Times Alphaville*. November 24, 2022:
https://www.ft.com/content/1eb245f9-ee69-4994-b37e-1c3152a48e83

Gwartney, James, Lawson, Robert, Hall, Joshua, and Murphy, Ryan. *Economic Freedom of the World 2022 Annual Report*. Fraser Institute. Available via:
https://www.fraserinstitute.org/sites/default/files/economic-freedom-of-the-world-2022.pdf

Hackle, Ekle. "You Never Change Things by Fighting the Existing Reality. To Change Something, Build a New Model that Makes the Existing Model Obsolete (Buckminster Fuller)." In *VIS-A-VIS Medien. Kunst.Bildung: Lebenswirklichkeiten und Kreative Potentiale der Digital Natives*, edited by Stefan Sonvilla-Weiss, 54–71. Berlin: De Gruyter, 2017.

Hafner, Katie *Where Wizards Stay Up Late: The Origins of the Internet*. Simon & Schuster: New York, 1998.

Harrison, Hope M. "Five Myths About the Berlin Wall." *Washington Post*. October 30, 2014:
https://www.washingtonpost.com/opinions/five-myths-about-the-berlin-wall/2014/10/30/f6cf1bc4-5df7-11e4-9f3a-7e28799e0549_story.html

Heinlein, Robert A. *The Moon Is a Harsh Mistress*. New York: Penguin, 1966.

Helms, Kevin. "Chinese Economist Says if Bitcoin Is Widely Adopted: 'We're All Going to Die, This Is Not a Joke'"

Bitcoin.com News. May 30, 2021:
https://news.bitcoin.com/chinese-economist-if-bitcoin-is-widely-adopted-were-all-going-to-die-this-is-not-a-joke/

Heywood, John. *The Proverbs, Epigrams, and Miscellanies of John Heywood*. Early English Drama Society: London, 1906.

History.com Editors, "Plessy v. Ferguson." October 29, 2009:
https://www.history.com/topics/black-history/plessy-v-ferguson

Hodges, Andrew. *Alan Turing: The Enigma: The Book That Inspired the Film* The Imitation Game, updated edition. Princeton University Press: Princeton, NJ., 2014.

Holloway, Vanessa. *Black Rights in the Reconstruction Era*. New York: Hamilton Press, 2018.

Holpuch, Amanda. "Chelsea Manning: I Leaked Reports After Seeing How Americans Ignored Wars." *The Guardian*. June 12, 2017:
https://www.theguardian.com/us-news/2017/jun/12/chelsea-manning-interview-leaked-documents

Holzer, Henry Mark. "How Americans Lost Their Right to Own Gold – and Became Criminals in the Process," *Brooklyn Law Review* 39, 3 (Winter 1973): 517–559.

Hossenfelder, Sabine. "Head Trip." *Scientific American* 313, 3 (September 2015): 46–49.

Hume, David. *An Enquiry Concerning Human Understanding. A Dissertation on the Passions. An Enquiry Concerning the Principles of Morals. The Natural History of Religion*. Vol 2. Edinburgh: T. Cadell; C. Elliot, T. Kay, and Company, 1788.

Internet Society. "Brief History of the Internet." Internet Society 20 Years, Jan 4, 2012. Available via:
https://www.albany.edu/faculty/dsaha/teach/2016Fall_CEN416/extraReading/Brief_History_of_the_Internet.pdf

Internet Society. "Internet Society Perspectives on Internet Content Blocking: An Overview," Measuring the Internet, March 24, 2017:
https://www.internetsociety.org/resources/doc/2017/internet-content-blocking/

Jevec, Adam. "'Semper Fidelis, Code Talkers'," *Prologue Magazine* 33, 4 (Winter 2001): https://www.archives.gov/publications/prologue/2001/winter/navajo-code-talkers.html

Jezard, Adam. "In 2020 Bitcoin Will Consume More Power Than the World Does Today." *World Economic Forum* December, 15 2017: https://www.weforum.org/agenda/2017/12/bitcoin-consume-more-power-than-world-2020/

Jobs, Steve. "Stanford Commencement Address." June 12, 2005. Available online via: https://lessons.unbounded.org/downloads/20794/pdf_proxy/ELA_6_Developing_Core_Proficiencies__Unit_2_EBC_Unit_Text.pdf

Johansen, Bruce E. *Forgotten Founders: Benjamin Franklin, the Iroquois and the Rationale for the American Revolution.* Gambit: Ipswich, Mass., 1982.

Kadar, Nicholas. "Rediscovering Ignaz Philipp Semmelweis (1818–1865)," *American Journal of Obstetrics and Gynecology* 220, 1 (January 2019): 26–39.

Khan Academy. "Creative Commons and Open Source." Available via: https://www.khanacademy.org/computing/computers-and-internet/xcae6f4a7ff015e7d:digital-information/xcae6f4a7ff015e7d:digital-copyright-and-licenses/a/creative-commons-and-open-source

Khan, Sal. "Education Reimagined." Stanford eCorner. April 16, 2014: https://ecorner.stanford.edu/wp-content/uploads/sites/2/2014/04/3315.pdf

Khan, Salman. *The One: Education Reimagined.* Twelve: New York, 2012.

Kiriya, Ilya and Sherstoboeva, Elena. "Russian Media Piracy in the Context of Censoring Practices," *International Journal of Communication* 9 (2015): 839–851.

Kocak, Korhan and Kıbrıs, Özgür. "Social Media and Press Freedom," *British Journal of Political Science* 53, 1 (January 2023): 140–162.

Komaromi, Ann. "Samizdat and Soviet Dissident Publics," *Slavic Review* 71, 1 (Spring 2012): 70–90.

Kowalewski, Stephen A., Blanton, Richard E., Feinman, Gary, and Finsten, Laura. "Boundaries, Scale, and Internal Organization," *Journal of Anthropological Archeology* 2, 1 (March 1983): 32–56.

Kraut, Richard. *Socrates and the State*. Princeton University Press: Princeton, NJ., 1984.

Kropotkin, Peter. "Anarchism." *Marxists.org*. First published in *The Encyclopædia Britannica*, 1910. Transcribed by Anarchy Archives: https://www.marxists.org/reference/archive/kropotkin-peter/1910/britannica.htm

Krugman, Paul. "Why Most Economists' Predictions are Wrong." *The Red Herring Magazine*. June 10, 1998. Available via WaybackMachine: https://web.archive.org/web/19980610100009/www.redherring.com/mag/issue55/economics.html

Lageman, Thessa. "Remembering Mohamed Bouazizi: The Man Who Sparked the Arab Spring." *Al Jazeera*. December 17, 2020: https://www.aljazeera.com/features/2020/12/17/remembering-mohamed-bouazizi-his-death-triggered-the-arab

Lamport, Leslie, Shostak, Robert, and Pease, Marshall. "The Byzantine Generals Problem," *ACM Transactions on Programming Languages and Systems* 4, 3 (1982): 382–401.

Langham, James. "Sir Isaac Newton," *Popular Astronomy* 55 (1947): 356–60.

Lee, Mike. *Written Out of History: The Forgotten Founders Who Fought Big Government*. Sentinel: New York, 2017.

Leiner, Barry Cerf, Vinton G., Clark, David D., Kahn, Robert E., Kleinrock, Leonard, Lynch, Daniel C., Postel, Jon, Roberts, Larry G., and Wolff, Stephen.

Library of Congress, "Revelations from the Russian Archives: Translation of Statistical Report." Committee of State Security of the USSR March 21, 1988 No. 458-Ch Moscow. Available via: https://www.loc.gov/exhibits/archives/trans-af2bdlit.html

Lih, Andrew. *The Wikipedia Revolution: How a Bunch of Nobodies Created the World's Greatest Encyclopedia.* Hyperion: New York, 2009.

Lindau, Juan D. Surveillance and the Vanishing Individual: Power and Privacy in the Digital Age. Rowman & Littlefield: Lanham, MD., 2023.

Linder, Doug. "The Trial of Socrates." SSRN manuscript, 2002. Available via: https://papers.ssrn.com/sol3/papers.cfm?abstract_id=1021249

Los Angeles Times. "The Lady's Not Made for Ducking a Tough Question." *Los Angeles Times Archives*, November 28, 1933. Available via: https://www.latimes.com/archives/la-xpm-1993-11-28-op-61920-story.html

Lowenstein, Roger. *America's Bank: The Epic Struggle to Create the Federal Reserve.* Penguin Press: New York, 2015.

Macmartin, Drew. "Hard to Soft Money: The Hyperinflation of the Roman Empire." *Bitcoin Magazine* Aug 5, 2021: https://bitcoinmagazine.com/culture/hard-money-hyperinflation-roman-empire

Major, Patrick. *Behind the Berlin Wall: East Germany and the Frontiers of Power.* Oxford: Oxford University Press, 2010.

Marchant, Jo. "A Journey to the Oldest Cave Paintings in the World." *Smithsonian Magazine.* January 2016: https://www.smithsonianmag.com/history/journey-oldest-cave-paintings-world-180957685/

Martin Luther King, Jr. "Letter From Birmingham Jail, Alabama, 16 April 1963." In *Oxford Essential Quotations*, sixth edition, edited by Susan Ratcliffe. New York, Oxford University Press, 2018. Available online via: https://www.oxfordreference.com/display/10.1093/acref/9780191866692.001.0001/q-oro-ed6-00006293

Martin, George R. R. *A Clash of Kings: The Illustrated Edition.* Book Two of A Song of Ice and Fire. Bantam Books: New York, 1999.

McBrayer, Gregory A. "Corrupting the Youth: Xenophon and Plato on Socrates and Alcibiades," *Kentron: Revue Pluridisciplinaire Du Monde Antique* 33 (2017): 75–90.

McNally, Danielle. "These Women Are the Last Thing Standing Between You and Nuclear War." Marie Claire, September 22, 2022: https://www.marieclaire.com/politics/air-force-nuclear-missileers/

McTighe, Kristen. "A Blogger at Arab Spring's Genesis." *The New York Times*. October 12, 2011: https://www.nytimes.com/2011/10/13/world/africa/a-blogger-at-arab-springs-genesis.html

Merton, Robert K. *On the Shoulders of Giants: A Shandean Postscript.* New York: The Free Press, 1965.

Milne, Joseph Grafton. "The Currency of Egypt Under the Ptolemies," *The Journal of Egyptian Archeology* 24, 1 (1938): 200–207.

Ministry of Information Industry. "Regulations on the Administration of Internet News Information Services," *Chinese Law & Government* 48, 2 (2016): 114–122.

Mitchell, Daniel J. "The Secret of Swiss Success Is Decentralization." *Fee.org.* July 2, 2016: https://fee.org/articles/the-secret-of-swiss-success-is-decentralization/

Moon, Jae Yun and Sproull, Lee. "Essence of Distributed Work: The Case of the Linux Kernel," *First Monday* 5, 11 (November 2000): https://firstmonday.org/ojs/index.php/fm/article/view/801/710

Musiani, Francesca. "Giants, Dwarfs and Decentralized Alternatives to Internet-based Services: An Issue of Internet Governance," *Westminster Papers in Communication and Culture* 10, 1 (2017): 81–94.

Naughtie, Andrew. "Did Bill Clinton Really 'Lose' the Nuclear Codes as Trump Claimed — and Does it Matter?" *The Independent.* October 11, 2022: https://www.independent.co.uk/news/world/americas/us-politics/bill-clinton-nuclear-codes-trump-b2200575.html

Naval History and Heritage Command. "Navajo Code Talkers' Dictionary." Revised June 15, 1945. Available via: https://www.history.navy.mil/research/library/online-reading-room/title-list-alphabetically/n/navajo-code-talker-dictionary.html

Naylor, Gloria. "The Meanings of a Word" [HERS Column], *The New York Times* February 20, 1986: https://www.nytimes.com/1986/02/20/garden/hers.html

Newton, Isaac. "Questiones Quædam Philosophiæ." The Newton Project, MS Add. 3996, Cambridge University Library, Cambridge, UK. Published online 2003: https://www.newtonproject.ox.ac.uk/view/texts/normalized/THEM00092

Newton, Matthew. "Is Linux Right For You?" *PCWorld* via CNN archive, April 5, 2000: https://edition.cnn.com/2000/TECH/computing/04/05/linux.you.idg/index.html

Nez, Chester and Avila, Judith Schiess. *Code Talker: The First and Only Memoir By One of the Original Navajo Code Talkers of WWII.* Berkley Caliber: New York, 2011.

Nieuwenhuijs, Jan, "Since Its Inception, the Euro Has Devalued by 85% Against Gold." Voima Gold, April 24, 2020: https://www.voimagold.com/releases/highlights/since-inception-the-euro-has-devalued-by-85-against-gold/

O'Toole, Garson. "Never Let Schooling Interfere With Your Education." Quote Investigator. September 25, 2010: https://quoteinvestigator.com/2010/09/25/schooling-vs-education/

Orwell, George. *1984*. Available via The Complete Works of George Orwell, George-Orwell.org: http://www.george-orwell.org/1984/6.html

Owen, Thomas C. "The Russian Industrial Society and Tsarist Economic Policy, 1867–1905," *Journal of Economic History* 45, 3 (1985): 587–606.

Paul, Ron. *The Case For Gold: Minority Report of the US Gold Commission 1982*. The Ludwig von Mises Institute: Auburn, Al., 2007.

Pease, Marshall, Shostak, Robert, and Lamport, Leslie. "Reaching Agreement in the Presence of Faults," *Journal of the Association for Computing Machinery* 27, 2 (April 1980): 228–234.

Pelley, Scott. "Fed Chair Jerome Powell's 60 Minutes Interview," *CBS News.* May 17, 2020. Available online via: https://www.cbsnews.com/news/full-transcript-fed-chair-jerome-powell-60-minutes-interview-economic-recovery-from-coronavirus-pandemic/

Pickrell, Ryan. "Trump's Erratic Presidency is the Latest Sign Giving One Person Control of the Nukes is 'Dangerous,' Experts Say." *Business Insider*, February 19, 2021: https://www.businessinsider.com/president-nuclear-weapon-command-authority-first-use-2021-2

Pilkington, Ed. "'Panic Made Us Vulnerable': How 9/11 Made the US Surveillance State – and the Americans Who Fought Back." *The Guardian.* September 4, 2021: https://www.theguardian.com/world/2021/sep/04/surveillance-state-september-11-panic-made-us-vulnerable

Plato, "The Apology of Socrates." Translated by Benjamin Jowett. The Center for Hellenic Studies, November 2, 2020: https://chs.harvard.edu/primary-source/plato-the-apology-of-socrates-sb/

Provoost, Sjors. *Bitcoin: A Work in Progress: Technical Innovations from the Trenches.* Purple Dunes, 2022.

Rand, Ayn. "The Nature of Government." *The Objectivist Newsletter* December 1963. Reprinted by *Freeman*, March 1, 1964. Accessible via Foundation for Economic Education: https://fee.org/articles/the-nature-of-government-by-ayn-rand/

Raymond, Eric S. *The Cathedral & the Bazaar: Musings on Linux and Open Source by an Accidental Revolutionary.* O'Reilly: Sebastopol, CA., 2001.

Robbins, Lionel. *An Essay on the Nature and Significance of Economic Science.* Macmillan & Co: London, 1932.

Rosenbaum, Ron. *How the End Begins: The Road to a Nuclear World War III.* Simon & Schuster: New York, 2012.

Rothman, Lily. "Wikipedia at 15: How the Concept of a Wiki Was Invented. *Time Magazine*. January 15, 2016: https://time.com/4177280/wiki-history-wikipedia/

Sandford, Christopher. *The Man Who Conned the World*. The History Press: Cheltenham, Gloucestershire, 2021.

Santayana, George. *The Life of Reason; or, The Phases of Human Progress*. Charles Scribner's Sons: New York, 1906.

Santos, Maria. "Not Even the Top 500 Supercomputers Combined Are More Powerful Than the Bitcoin Network." *99Bitcoins.com*. January 2, 2018: https://99bitcoins.com/not-even-the-top-500-supercomputers-combined-are-more-powerful-than-the-bitcoin-network

Service, Robert. *The Last of the Tsars: Nicholas II and the Russian Revolution*. Macmillan: London, 2017.

Seth, Michael J. *A History of Korea: From Antiquity to the Present*. Rowman & Littlefield: Plymouth, U.K., 2011.

Shaw, George Bernard. "The Author's Apology," in *Mrs. Warren's Profession*. Brentano's: New York, 1905.

Shoemaker, Nancy. "The Rise or Fall of Iroquois Women," *Journal of Women's History* 2, 3 (Winter 1991): 39–57.

Sieroń, Arkadiusz. *Money, Inflation and Business Cycles: The Cantillon Effect and the Economy*. Routledge: Abingdon, Oxon, 2019.

Simmons, John Galbraith. *Doctors and Discoveries: Lives That Created Today's Medicine*. Boston: Houghton Mifflin Company, 2002.

Singh, Manish. "Wikipedia Now Has More Than 6 Million Articles in English." *TechCrunch*, January 24, 2020: https://techcrunch.com/2020/01/23/wikipedia-english-six-million-articles/

Skilling, H. Gordon. *Samizdat and an Independent Society in Central and Eastern Europe*. Macmillan Press: London, 1989.

Snowden, Edward. *Terminal F/Chasing Edward Snowden (2015),* documentary, January 13, 2005. Available via: https://youtu.be/Nd6qN167wKo?t=555

Snyder, Timothy. *Bloodlands: Europe Between Hitler and Stalin.* Allen Lane: New York, 2010.

Sowell, Thomas. *Is Reality Optional? And Other Essays.* Hoover Institution Press: Stanford, CA., 1993.

Sowell, Thomas. *The Vision of the Anointed: Self-Congratulation as a Basis for Social Policy.* Basic Books: New York, 1995.

St. Onge, Peter. Personal correspondence with the author, May 3, 2023.

Stallman, Richard. "Free Software, Free Society." *TEDx Geneva.* June 13, 2014: https://youtu.be/Ag1AKIl_2GM?t=10 (0:10–0:18).

Stallman, Richard. "Free Unix!" September 27, 1983. Available via GNU Operating System: https://www.gnu.org/gnu/initial-announcement.en.html

State Council. "Regulations for the Protection and Management of the International Networking of Computer Information Networks," Chinese Law & Government 48, 1 (2016): 60–64.

Stewart, Potter. *Ginzburg v. United States*, 383 U.S. 463 (1966), dissenting: 383 U.S. 498: https://supreme.justia.com/cases/federal/us/383/463/

Stueck, William. "The Korean War." In *The Cambridge History of the Cold War*, edited by Melvyn P. Leffler and Odd Arne Westad, 266–287. Cambridge: Cambridge University Press, 2010.

Svanholm, Knut. *Bitcoin: Everything Divided by 21 Million.* Konsensus Network.

Swaim, Barton. "'Trust, But Verify': An Untrustworthy Political Phrase." *Washington Post.* March 11, 2016: https://www.washingtonpost.com/opinions/trust-but-verify-an-untrustworthy-political-phrase/2016/03/11/da32fb08-db3b-11e5-891a-4ed04f4213e8_story.html

Taylor, Telford. *Munich: The Price of Peace.* Doubleday: Garden City, N.Y., 1979.

Tekaroniake Evans, Tony. "How the Iroquois Confederacy Was Formed." *History.com* November 8, 2021: https://www.history.com/news/iroquois-confederacy-hiawatha-peacemaker-great-law-of-peace

Thoreau, Henry David. "Civil Disobedience." In *The Essays of Henry David Thoreau*, edited by Richard Dillman: 16–34. NCUP: Albany, NY., 1990.

Tibballs, Geoff. *I Wish I Hadn't Said That: Over 3,000 Famous Foot-in-Mouth Moments*. Little, Brown: London, 2019.

Torvalds, Linus. "Notes for Linux Release 0.01." Available via: https://mirrors.edge.kernel.org/pub/linux/kernel/Historic/old-versions/RELNOTES-0.01

Torvalds, Linus. "Software is Like Sex: It's Better When it's Free." *Twitter*, January 29, 2013: https://twitter.com/Linus__Torvalds/status/296333253571387392

Veenendaal, Wouter. "The Curious Case of Liechtenstein: A Country Caught Between a Prince and Democracy." *LSE Blog.* January 30, 2017: https://blogs.lse.ac.uk/europpblog/2017/01/30/the-curious-case-of-liechtenstein/

Walsh, Colleen. "Education Without Limits," *The Harvard Gazette.* May 9, 2013: https://news.harvard.edu/gazette/story/2013/05/education-without-limits/

Wikipedia. "Copyleft." Accessed May 7, 2023: https://en.wikipedia.org/wiki/Copyleft

Wikipedia. "Free and Open-Source Software." Accessed May 7, 2023: https://en.wikipedia.org/wiki/Free_and_open-source_software

Wikipedia. "Reliability of Wikipedia." Accessed May 7, 2023: https://en.wikipedia.org/wiki/Reliability_of_Wikipedia

Wiktionary. "Consensus" entry. Available via: https://en.wiktionary.org/wiki/consensus#Etymology

Williams, Sam. *Free as in Freedom: Richard Stallman's Crusade for Free Software*. O'Reilly: Sebastopol, CA., 2002.

Wilson, Emily R. *The Death of Socrates*. Harvard University Press: Cambridge, Mass., 2007.

Wirdum, Aaron van. "The Genesis Files: How David Chaim's eCash Spawned a Cypherpunk dream." *Bitcoin Magazine*. April 28, 2018: https://bitcoinmagazine.com/culture/genesis-files-how-david-chaums-ecash-spawned-cypherpunk-dream

Wohlgemuth, Michael. "Liechtenstein: A Tale of Unusual Sovereignty." Stiftung für Staatsrecht und Ordnungspolitik, June 2021. Available via: https://sous.li/wp-content/uploads/2021/06/Liechtenstein-sovereignty-for-SOuS-4.pdf

Wood, John H. *A History of Central Banking in Great Britain and the United States*. Cambridge University Press: New York, 2005.

World Bank. "Financial Inclusion on the Rise, But Gaps Remain, Global Findex Database Shows." Press Release NO: 2018/130/DEC. April 19, 2018: https://www.worldbank.org/en/news/press-release/2018/04/19/financial-inclusion-on-the-rise-but-gaps-remain-global-findex-database-shows

Yamargata, Hiroo. "The Pragmatist of Free Software: Linus Torvalds Interview." Conducted for hotWIRED Japan, September 20, 1997. Available online via: https://www.tech-insider.org/linux/research/1997/0920.html

Zhang., Xinyao "Centralization and Corruption: The Political Dilemma of the Late Roman Empire," *Advances in Social Science, Education and Humanities Research* 664: 1481–1485.

Zimbardo, Philip and Boyd, John. *The Time Paradox: The New Psychology of Time That Will Change Your Life*. Free Press: New York, 2008.

Zimmer, Oliver. *Forging the Swiss Nation, 1760–1939: Popular Memory, Patriotic Invention and Competing Conceptions of Nationhood*. PhD Thesis, London School of Economics, 1999.

Zittrain, Jonathan. "Technology Lessons from the Wikileaks Saga." *MIT Technology Review*. August 4, 2010:

https://www.technologyreview.com/2010/08/04/201712/technology-lessons-from-the-wikileaks-saga/

Zubieta, Leslie F. "The Role of Rock Art as a Mnemonic Device in the Memorisation of Cultural Knowledge." In *The Role of Rock Art as a Mnemonic Device in the Memorisation of Cultural Knowledge*, edited by Leslie F. Zubieta: 77–98. Springer: Cham, Switzerland, 2022.

Zuckoff, Mitchell. *Ponzi's Scheme: The True Story of a Financial Legend*. Random House: New York, 2005.